# NASCAR®

## by Brian Tarcy

# ALPHA

A member of Penguin Group (USA) Inc.

*For my mother, Dorothy Tarcy, and my late father, Paul Tarcy.*

## ALPHA BOOKS

Published by the Penguin Group

Penguin Group (USA) Inc., 375 Hudson Street, New York, New York 10014, USA

Penguin Group (Canada), 90 Eglinton Avenue East, Suite 700, Toronto, Ontario M4P 2Y3, Canada (a division of Pearson Penguin Canada Inc.)

Penguin Books Ltd, 80 Strand, London WC2R 0RL, England

Penguin Ireland, 25 St. Stephen's Green, Dublin 2, Ireland (a division of Penguin Books Ltd.)

Penguin Group (Australia), 250 Camberwell Road, Camberwell, Victoria 3124, Australia (a division of Pearson Australia Group Pty. Ltd.)

Penguin Books India Pvt. Ltd., 11 Community Centre, Panchsheel Park, New Delhi—110 017, India

Penguin Group (NZ), 67 Apollo Drive, Rosedale, North Shore, Auckland 1311, New Zealand (a division of Pearson New Zealand Ltd.)

Penguin Books (South Africa) (Pty.) Ltd, 24 Sturdee Avenue, Rosebank, Johannesburg 2196, South Africa

Penguin Books Ltd., Registered Offices: 80 Strand, London WC2R 0RL, England

## Copyright © 2008 by Brian Tarcy

International Standard Book Number: 978-1-59257-697-5
Library of Congress Catalog Card Number: 2007932652

10  09  08      8  7  6  5  4  3  2  1

Interpretation of the printing code: The rightmost number of the first series of numbers is the year of the book's printing; the rightmost number of the second series of numbers is the number of the book's printing. For example, a printing code of 08-1 shows that the first printing occurred in 2008.

*Printed in the United States of America*

**Note:** This publication contains the opinions and ideas of its author. It is intended to provide helpful and informative material on the subject matter covered. It is sold with the understanding that the author and publisher are not engaged in rendering professional services in the book. If the reader requires personal assistance or advice, a competent professional should be consulted.

The author and publisher specifically disclaim any responsibility for any liability, loss, or risk, personal or otherwise, which is incurred as a consequence, directly or indirectly, of the use and application of any of the contents of this book.

This publication has not been prepared, approved, endorsed, or authorized by the National Association for Stock Car Auto Racing.

Most Alpha books are available at special quantity discounts for bulk purchases for sales promotions, premiums, fund-raising, or educational use. Special books, or book excerpts, can also be created to fit specific needs.

For details, write: Special Markets, Alpha Books, 375 Hudson Street, New York, NY 10014.

**Publisher:** *Marie Butler-Knight*
**Editorial Director:** *Mike Sanders*
**Managing Editor:** *Billy Fields*
**Acquisitions Editor:** *Michele Wells*
**Development Editor:** *Julie Bess*
**Senior Production Editor:** *Janette Lynn*

**Copy Editor:** *Ross Patty*
**Cover Designer:** *Bill Thomas*
**Book Designer:** *Trina Wurst*
**Indexer:** *Angie Bess*
**Layout:** *Ayanna Lacey*
**Proofreader:** *Mary Hunt*

# Contents at a Glance

# Contents

# Foreword

Racing is in my blood. When I was 16 years old my Mom, by herself, helped me change an engine. It was fun working with her, although she was shocked to learn that I knew a cuss word. Speed thrilled me. As a teenager I'd work on cars in my uncle's barn and then pull them to the racetrack by a chain because we didn't have a trailer. We wanted to be there. And I wanted to learn everything as fast as possible.

I thought of this when I was asked to look at this book. It made me recall how my Dad introduced me to racing. I remember my Dad telling stories and showing me how things are done—done right. So when I got a chance to look at this book, which just might be your introduction to racing, I found a fact-filled fun product that explains NASCAR in simple yet complete terms—a fun read with great photos.

This book made me think of my brother and sister and how they supported me. It reminded me that, above all, NASCAR is a family sport. From when I was young, I've always loved the roar of the engines and I felt at home at the track.

My first job in racing was at BoLaws and later I worked with Ray Stonkus, who generously shared his considerable wisdom. Along the way I was honored to learn many of life's lessons from Richard Petty and Dale Inman, and equally honored that Jeff Gordon believed in me and always helped me reach for more. That's NASCAR. NASCAR is family; my extended family—the people who have been there through the heartaches and victories of life.

And that NASCAR family includes you, the fans. That's why I like this book so much. It reaches out. It explains. And yes, it gives glory where glory is due. Sure, this is *The Complete Idiot's Guide to NASCAR.* But you are no idiot to buy it. In fact, you are smart to buy this book, the easiest and most fun introduction to NASCAR anywhere.

See you in Victory Lane!

Robbie Loomis
Director of Racing
Petty Enterprises

# Introduction

The first thing I did when I was asked to write this book was drink beer ... with my friend Tammy, who is a smart, passionate NASCAR fan. You see, this is a Complete Idiot's Guide and I am a complete idiot. But I am no ordinary idiot. I am a professional.

And I am not only the author of this book; I am also the audience. I drove my Chevy into this project knowing less about NASCAR than you do and then I found passionate fans such as Tammy Cunniff, and professionals inside of the sport such as legendary crew chief Robbie Loomis who were willing to answer my stupid questions. They helped, I learned, and as I did I learned to love.

It's like this; I am a sports fan—I live and breathe for my favorite football and baseball teams (Cleveland Browns and Cleveland Indians). But when the black "07" Jack Daniels Chevrolet crossed the finish line in 18th place of the 2007 Daytona 500 while upside down and on fire, and then the driver, Clint Bowyer, exited and casually tossed his gloves into the burning vehicle, I found a new passion.

Upside down and on fire across the finish line in a Jack Daniels car— I dare any sport to top that.

This is a research project and more. I know how to ask stupid questions and so I asked. And that began the education of me, who is here to teach you all the stuff that they—and they, especially my photographer, Bryan Hallman, are an incredible group—taught me.

So I kept asking stupid questions. Along the way, I became interested, fascinated, and then enamored. I bet you do, too.

The organization of this book is simple—I aim to teach you what I have learned about the great sport of NASCAR—step by step:

- ◆ Why is it cool?
- ◆ How did it start?
- ◆ What is it basically about?
- ◆ The 36-race season
- ◆ The different tracks

- The car
- The strategy
- The driver
- The pit crew
- The business side
- Legends and lore
- The cultural phenomenon

My aim is to explain NASCAR to you—not just how it works, but why it works. The sport is as simple as *turn left, finish first*—or as complex as an infinite equation.

So follow this book chapter by chapter—the plot is fascinating, full of heroes and villains—or just jump around and learn as you go. There is plenty of information throughout the book on the many aspects of NASCAR.

NASCAR is the fastest growing sport in America. Here's why.

## Extras

Throughout the book, you'll find a number of definitions and bits of lore and information in the form of sidebars and margin notes designed to help answer questions and illuminate the world of NASCAR.

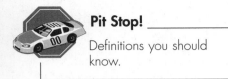

**Pit Stop!**
Definitions you should know.

**Awesome!**
Stories, NASCAR lore, and other interesting facts.

## Acknowledgments

My learning curve on this project had NASCAR acceleration, and lots of help. Thank you especially …

Bryan Hallman was my photographer and technical reviewer. Your kindness amazed me, your knowledge impressed me, and your photos are awesome. My first tutor was a friend and race fan, Tammy Cunniff, who drives a Mustang in streetcar drag races. Another friend, NASCAR fanatic Jonathan Wasseth, continued my education and invited me to his Daytona 500 party where his friends furthered my understanding of the sport they love. Thanks to all.

Others helped along the way, including Audrey Hackett, a former journalistic insider; John Taylor, football writer for theobr.com; and Jim Power, former "voice of the track" at a number of New England tracks. Thanks for your valuable input.

Art Weinstein, managing editor of NASCAR Scene, taught me about the Nextel Cup season; Breon Klopp, senior director of development at PIT Instruction and Training, taught me about pit crews; Dick Berggren, legendary editor of *Speedway Illustrated Magazine* and TV analyst, as well as Robbie Loomis, legendary crew chief and current Director of Race Operations for Petty Racing, helped me understand race strategy; and Jon Ackley and Mike Pitts of Virginia Commonwealth University gave me NASCAR business lessons. I'd like to thank my agent, Mike Snell, and my editor, Michele Wells, for believing in me; and my great mechanic, Paul Siegmund, for fixing my car at my deadline. And thanks to my development editor Julie Bess and technical editor John Bavaro, who helped me appear smarter than I am.

I'd like to thank my friends for putting up with me, especially Bob Vander Pyle and Steve "Otis" O'Kernick. Thanks to my favorite band, "Plan B" of Woods Hole, Massachusetts, for the best original songs in the world. Thanks to Frank and Joyce Gallagher for the random humor and car wash, Dan Ring for the Boston sports news updates, and always thanks to Paul and Heidi Perekrests—for everything.

Thank you Laura Reckford for arriving in my life just as I entered the world of NASCAR. Your writing inspired me, while your sense of humor, optimism, and sweet smile kept me going (4Ls). I'd like to thank my mother, Dorothy, and my two brothers, Gary and Dave, for everything through history including, you know, not kicking me out of the family.

Finally and most important, my kids make every day a trip to Victory Lane. Thank you Denim, Derek, Kayli, and Marissa. You are the best ever.

## Special Thanks to the Technical Editor and Reviewer

*The Complete Idiot's Guide to NASCAR* was reviewed by an expert who double-checked the accuracy of what you'll learn here, to help us ensure that this book gives you everything you need to know about NASCAR. Special thanks are extended to John Bavaro.

Extra special thanks to Bryan Hallman, who served as technical reviewer and a source of knowledge throughout the writing of this book.

## Trademarks

All terms mentioned in this book that are known to be or are suspected of being trademarks or service marks have been appropriately capitalized. Alpha Books and Penguin Group (USA) Inc. cannot attest to the accuracy of this information. Use of a term in this book should not be regarded as affecting the validity of any trademark or service mark.

# Chapter 1

# That Looks Like My Car, Sort Of

## In This Chapter

- ◆ A look at the appeal of speed
- ◆ What is and what isn't a stock car
- ◆ An explanation of NASCAR as a contact sport
- ◆ The continuing story/soap opera aspect of NASCAR

Imagine driving almost 200-mph in bumper-to-bumper traffic. Now imagine driving like that in your own car. Talk about rush hour.

This is a book about the world of NASCAR (National Association for Stock Car Automobile Racing)—big-time automobile racing in which the cars look like yours, sort of. And that's why, if you watch for even a little while, it's easy to imagine yourself driving one of these cars.

Let's say you are driving from Cleveland to New York City (or, if you'd like, New Orleans to Dallas) in this kind of inches-away wild traffic and for all 500 miles 42 other stubborn, road-rage-waiting-to-happen drivers around you will do most anything to get there first—including team up, even with you. Imagine a crossroads where technology meets human skill. Your hands are on the wheel and your scruples are on display. For some reason, this route has a lot of left turns, millions of people are watching and, oh yeah, corporate America has placed a very large bet on you getting there first. Plus, get this—there could be a fiery sedan-flipping crash at any instant and you might have no choice but to be part of it. Yes, people have died doing this. Others have found incredible glory. Some have found both. Inches away. Are your palms sweating yet?

In this opening chapter, you'll get an introduction to the appeal of all kinds of racing as well as a basic explanation of NASCAR racing, which is a specific kind of automobile racing featuring cars that look like yours.

# Everybody Loves Racing—Speed Always Thrills

The urge to race, to see who can go fastest, has always existed. From running races in the ancient Olympics to horseraces to chariot races to, heck, anything imaginable, contests of speed have always been part of the human experience. Cars just took it to a whole new level.

**Awesome!**

Richard Petty, the greatest driver in the history of NASCAR, once said, "There is no doubt about precisely when folks began racing each other in automobiles. It was the day they built the second automobile."

Cars and speed are a mythic part of American culture. You don't have to get anywhere near the big events to understand that automobiles and America go together. And when you throw the word "fast" into the mix, it naturally ups the ante.

Fast cars. Think about it.

*(Courtesy of Bryan Hallman.)*

*Speed is exciting.*

Those two little words bring a million images to mind—songs and movies, and maybe even scenes from your own life. Put them together and they mean so much more than just fast and cars.

A big engine, spinning tires, and a little bit of grease say things to each of us. What is it? That's up to you but to almost all of us, an automobile is more than just a piece of technology. A car is somehow alive.

The horror author Stephen King once made a car come alive in one of his books and it worked because King is brilliant but also because we Americans have a special relationship with our automobiles. We understood. It seemed plausible. So it is only natural that our competitive nature as humans would come through in our cars.

# There's Speed and Then There's NASCAR Speed

Of course, if all of us drove as if there were a million-dollar prize waiting for us, there could be a bit of havoc on the American roadway.

Thus, in real life, there must be rules. But rules have never stopped humans from figuring a way to do what they want, so along the way (more on this in Chapter 2) racetracks were invented and in 1947

NASCAR, the organizing body for stock car racing, was born. The theory was that racing was too dangerous for the real roads. But no one was going to stop racing, so why not put it on a track away from everyone else? Of course, people were interested in watching, too. And they remain so.

Putting cars on racetracks was a brilliant idea, and then organizing all the different racetracks so they had similar rules was the point of the formation of NASCAR. But the real point was speed. Pure and simple. People want to see speed and wherever there is a racetrack, speed is on display. Of course, speed exists in many different realms and "fast" is a relative concept even if you just think about cars.

There are many kinds of automobile racing. NASCAR involves stock cars.

# What Is a Stock Car?

The simple definition of a stock car is that it is the kind of car you would find in stock at your local automobile dealer's showroom.

It's not a real definition anymore, but it used to be. Now, the cars racing in NASCAR just sort of look like the cars in stock at a dealer's showroom, and they have the same name. But you can't really go down to the local dealership and get one of those cars. You only wish you could.

If you are new to automobile racing, you may have heard of other kinds of racing, too, and maybe not realized that all of it is different. Well, it is.

Essentially, automobile racing is split into closed-wheeled and open-wheeled vehicles. A stock car is closed-wheeled—in other words the fender covers the wheel so that it is not outside of the car. Open-wheeled vehicles have open cockpits and the wheels stick out and are not covered by a fender. They look very different than stock cars.

Here is what stock car racing isn't:

## Stock Car Racing Isn't Drag Racing

Although stock cars could be used in a drag race, these short, straight-line races are typically done with specialty cars that are so fast they need parachutes to help slow the vehicles at the end of the race.

A drag race is usually one-quarter mile long. The biggest organization in drag racing is the National Hot Rod Association (NHRA). Although drag racing is very exciting, races last a very short time and they don't have the extended drama of a NASCAR race.

## Stock Car Racing Isn't Formula One

Formula One (a.k.a. F1) racing is single-seat, open-wheeled racing with the top technology and aerodynamics in the world. Formula One racing, done mostly outside of the United States, involves cars that are significantly faster than NASCAR vehicles, but because of the open-wheeled design, do not have any of the bumping of NASCAR.

Formula One drivers participate in *Grand Prix* races. Famous F1 drivers have included Jackie Stewart, Michael Schumacher, and Mario Andretti.

**Pit Stop!**

**Grand Prix** means grand prize. In Formula One racing, the Grand Prix is the premier race in any given nation. The first Grand Prix was held in Le Mans, France, in 1906.

Although there is some F1 racing done in the United States, a more prevalent form of open-wheeled racing in America is Indy Car racing.

## Stock Car Racing Isn't Indy Car Racing

The Indianapolis 500 runs cars that look very much like Formula One cars but they are called Indy Cars—designed for a counterclockwise oval. In other words, they look the same and are about as fast but the steering is a bit different. Indy cars turn left whereas F1 cars run on road races and, thus, have to turn both left and right equally well.

Indy car racing in the United States has become very political in recent years and there are now two different sanctioning bodies. The Championship Auto Racing Teams (CART) organization represents many major races for Indy cars. The Indy Racing League (IRL) runs the Indianapolis 500.

*(Courtesy of Bryan Haltman.)*

*An open-wheeled Indy car.*

Famous Indy Car drivers have included A. J. Foyt, Al Unser, Bobby Unser, Emerson Fittipaldi, and Al Unser Jr.

# Comparing F1/Indy and NASCAR

Fans of the two sports (F1/Indy Car racing and NASCAR racing) tend to make fun of the other sport. NASCAR fans think there is too much reliance on technology in F1/Indy Car racing and F1 fans make fun of NASCAR for keeping so much technology from the 1950s. Both are exaggerations, and the funny thing is, there seems to be some mutual respect between Formula One drivers and NASCAR drivers.

There is even some crossover. Juan Pablo Montoya has raced in F1 and Indy cars, picking up wins in the Le Mans Grand Prix and the Indianapolis 500 along the way. In 2007, amid much media hoopla, Montoya made the jump into NASCAR.

And although no NASCAR driver has made the jump into F1/Indy car racing, it doesn't mean the drivers don't envy the technology. "I am just beyond belief when I look at them," NASCAR driver Kurt Busch told *The Wall Street Journal* in 2005. "I'd love to have the opportunity to drive one."

Although NASCAR drivers often look at the advanced technology and even the exotic race locations with some envy, they still know that NASCAR is the most exciting, action-packed type of racing.

Sure, F1 cars are half as heavy and have more horsepower so they go faster. But NASCAR features more close finishes, more lead changes, and, best of all, drivers challenging each other and banging around out on the racecourse.

# A Little Crashin' & Bangin' (Trading Paint)

NASCAR racing is a contact sport. Crashes or near crashes are, in fact, common and even expected in every race. And that, more than anything else, just might explain the true appeal of stock car racing as opposed to any other kind of automobile racing.

On any given Sunday, NASCAR is liable to turn into a high-speed demolition derby. Even when it doesn't, it often looks like it is just about to happen. Cars racing at incredible speeds inches away from each other tend to give that effect. And yes, it's cool. Very cool.

*(Courtesy of Bryan Hallman.)*

*Tradin' paint at incredible speed.*

That's part of the appeal of it. It fits that word—it's cool. It's cool because it's awesome, it's tremendous, it's dangerous and exciting and all those words put together plus a few more that add up to a NASCAR race with the excitement that comes with the phrase, "you never know."

As cars circle a track that is anywhere from a half-mile to 2 1/2 miles long, they are running at incredible speeds with variable traction and aerodynamics. Running alone, there is the possibility of something going wrong. Add in 42 other cars with skilled and ruthless drivers and the odds of *the big one* happening go up.

> **Pit Stop!**
>
> **The big one** refers to the almost inevitable multiple-car pileup that happens, especially at the long superspeedways of Talladega and Daytona. Cars are so close together that when a crash happens, sometimes more than 20 cars are involved.

And that's a big part of how the dramatics of a race begin to take shape. Will it happen? When will it happen? A driver doesn't want to be in the middle of it. It's best to be at the front. Or the back. Or …

A driver doesn't really know where to be because it could happen any time in a 500-mile race, and although you get some points for leading a lap (more in Chapter 4) the most important time to be in front is at the end of the race. All the drivers know the same thing.

So all drivers aim to get to the same place first. Back and forth the battle ensues. And yes, it is a battle because the cars don't just race. They challenge each other. Time and again cars block and cars challenge. Back and forth, all through the field this is happening.

It is not unusual for a car to get banged up a little and continue on. These cars sometimes touch each other and sometimes drivers accuse each other of deliberately running a car off the track or worse, even into a wall.

Stock car racing is not a sport for the timid. Winners are fearless—and lucky. Cars often bump side to side (*tradin' paint*) and the challenge is for both drivers to maintain control while both also vie for a superior position.

> **Pit Stop!**
>
> **Tradin' paint** occurs when two cars bump but don't have a major collision. Often, there is actually paint from one car on the body of the other.

And this goes on and on—round and round like some sort of high-speed boxing match or game of chicken. Maybe the red car with the beer logo is banging up against the black car with the logo for the chain of home goods stores. Maybe five other cars with five other colorful corporate logos are involved in the same sort of tussle and maybe it's even more complicated than that because lots of cars are having lots of different battles.

And there is strategy. Cars can work together or against each other and this kind of cooperation can even change lap to lap. In the end, of course, all drivers want to win. A million things go into the equation of who wins, and most of it truly has to do with the car itself. However, it's the melding of man and machine that makes a winner. When the driver challenges the car, the car must respond and when it bangs into another car, the driver expects the car to hold its own.

And the tension increases as the race goes on. Although crashes can happen at any time in a race, they seem most common at the end of a race when everything is on the line and it's now-or-never time.

# The 2007 Daytona 500

The 49th Daytona 500, on February 18, 2007, was one of the most dramatic races in NASCAR history and it had a good share of crashin' and bangin' and tradin' paint.

Starting in 34th position was the eventual winner, Kevin Harvick's yellow Shell/Penzoil No. 29 car, who worked his way to a .02 second victory over longtime favorite Mark Martin's black U.S. Army No. 01 car. But as dramatic as that victory was, with Harvick mounting a furious charge out of the final turn, there was even more excitement right behind them.

Drivers were still vying for position because a driver gets more points for finishing closer to the front. Matt Kenseth, Kyle Bush, and Jeff Gordon were all bumping and trying to get the best position when suddenly it all broke loose and within seconds Clint Bowyer's black Jack Daniels Chevrolet was upside down, on fire, and crossing the *start/finish line*.

**Pit Stop!**

The **start/finish line** is the checkered line that signals where cars start and is also where the race ends—thus the name.

Bowyer was fine and even got out of the car calmly, after it flipped right side up, and then tossed his gloves into the burning car in disgust.

*(Courtesy of Kevin Thorne.)*

*Clint Bowyer calmly gets out of his burning car just after it crossed the 2007 Daytona 500 start/finish line upside down and on fire. The car finally rolled to right-side up.*

It was another NASCAR moment, and in an odd way, with the liquor logo and the tragic end of the flipping, on-fire vehicle, it harkened back to the earliest era of stock car racing (see Chapter 2) when cars were built fast to haul bootleg liquor and were forced to drive fast to get away from police. Bowyer, unlike some illegal bootleggers and even NASCAR drivers, emerged from his car unhurt. In fact, he finished in 18th place.

Even earlier in the race, a crash figured prominently as the leaders with 47 laps to go, Tony Stewart and Kurt Busch, crashed and both were knocked out of the race with damaged cars.

For the most part, because of incredible safety advances (more in Chapter 6), the cars get hurt in the crashes, but not the drivers. It's still a very dangerous sport, but not as dangerous as it used to be. But it may be even more exciting.

# This Is a Sport So Pick a Team—Yes, a Team

NASCAR fans have favorites and loyalties that run deep. And although much of the focus is on the driver, there is sometimes—though not always—a lot more that goes into the complicated algorithm that produces fan loyalty.

So look around, watch a couple of races. You'll figure it out. Start by paying attention to the drivers and the way they drive and whether you agree with their style or not. Style of driving? Yes, keep reading, there's a lot more about that in the chapters to come.

But there is more to it than just the driver. Wait. More to it than the driver? Like what?

- **The make of the car.** Three companies have raced in NASCAR for years—Ford, Chevrolet, and Dodge. In 2007, Toyota entered Sprint Cup Racing—which is the highest level of NASCAR racing (for more on the Sprint Cup season, see Chapter 4).

**Awesome!**

In July 2007, it was announced that the name of the top series was changed from the Nextel Cup to the Sprint Cup effective starting the 2008 season.

- **The main sponsor of the car.** Do you like M&Ms, or Dupont Paint, Budweiser? These are just a few of the corporate logos that race on Sundays.

- **The owner.** Each owner has a different personality and brings technical skills, know-how, and money to the team.

- **The pit crew.** The folks that work on the car during breaks in the race, and especially the crew chief, are a public face of the team during a competition.

And yet, inevitably it all comes back to the driver because the driver, well, drives the car.

# Drivers Are Celebrities and the Story Continues

NASCAR is a hero machine.

Some might have you believe that NASCAR is not a major sport compared to the major sports of football, baseball, and basketball. On the other hand, in the places where NASCAR is a major sport, it is often *the* major sport.

And in modern NASCAR, a driver does much more than simply drive the car. A driver represents dreams.

As with fans of almost anything, fans of NASCAR live vicariously. The heroes and villains are on display from race to race, and week to week. Storylines begin to play out:

Remember that crash from last week? Did you see who caused it? Everyone else did. Gosh, I wonder what's going to happen this week.

And drivers work for owners, but sometimes they switch teams.

Plus some guys are just easy for many fans to hate. Why? The answers vary as much as the fans and the drivers. And as NASCAR has grown in popularity and, thus, coverage, the personalities of the drivers have become even more visible.

Some drivers do commercials and talk show appearances and all drivers are interviewed and examined endlessly by all sorts of media. And because there are so few drivers, all aspects of their lives are examined. If one driver's wife is having a baby, will it affect how he races? If another is having problems with the owner, will that affect how he races? Stay tuned.

## The Least You Need to Know

- The urge to race has always existed and car racing was a natural evolution.
- Stock cars look something like your car but Indy Cars don't.
- In NASCAR racing, cars sometimes bump against each other.
- Drivers are larger-than-life celebrities and NASCAR is a story.

# Chapter 2

# The History of NASCAR

## In This Chapter

◆ The bootlegging roots

◆ Bill France and the formation of NASCAR

◆ Early NASCAR, from dirt tracks to superspeedways

◆ The Winston Cup and the modern era

◆ The Sprint Cup

Stock car racing wasn't so much born as it was fermented until it was ready for mass consumption. Although racing most likely occurred wherever folks had automobiles, it began to catch fire in the 1930s in the southeastern United States because of, well, moonshine. That's right, moonshine. It's a sort of funny, only-in-America kind of story but this one is even more local.

The simplified version goes like this: the moonshiners had stills in the mountains. The customers (and there were lots of customers) were in the cities. In between the moonshiners and the customers were downhill, crazy winding roads and maybe the law, waiting to catch someone transporting illegal, untaxed moonshine. There weren't always chases but there were enough of them to cause the drivers to work on their cars.

And then after the run, perhaps fueled by the product in question, the drivers sat around and talked—sometimes about how fast their vehicles were.

*"Mine's faster."*

*"No way, mine is."*

*"Prove it!"*

The earliest records of the first racing conversation are lost, but an educated guess says it probably went just like that. This is a chapter about what is known about the origins of the sport and its subsequent growth.

# Bootlegging and Bragging

Untaxed alcohol is illegal in America, and in a way that's how this all started. The makers of moonshine didn't want to pay taxes and the government wasn't happy about it. So a cat-and-mouse game was born.

The truth is that racing was occurring all over America. Wherever a county fair popped up, most likely a track was built to accommodate a race. But in the southeastern United States, racing evolved out of business practices and in an odd way, it was the American entrepreneurial spirit that fueled it.

As the long-repeated legend has it, corn liquor (a.k.a. moonshine) has always been a good, homegrown business that the government has been trying to tax.

**Awesome!** _____

Maybe George Washington is responsible for NASCAR. In 1794, farmers in western Pennsylvania were violently protesting a tax on whiskey. Washington, as sitting president (just imagine!) led 13,000 men to stop "the Whiskey Rebellion." Two rebels were sentenced to die but Washington pardoned both, because one was a "simpleton" and the other was "insane." Since then, untaxed whiskey making has fled to the hills.

When moonshine was chased underground, a new business was born of trying to get the untaxed liquor to those who wanted it. By the 1930s, as cars were becoming advanced, drivers began fixing up their cars—adding extra springs in the back to carry the weight of the booze, and adding extra engine power to keep ahead of any lawman that might aspire for a chase.

On the other side of the law, all up and down the spine of the Appalachian Mountains, sat lawmen just trying to do their job. They inevitably fixed up their cars some, too. Just not quite as much as the moonshiners.

The game was on. And though it was rarely violent, it was serious, and the speeds that cars achieved on winding mountain roads could send them plummeting to their deaths. Or sometimes the bootleggers got caught and went to jail. But more often than not, the liquor and driver arrived safely at the destination and sometimes there was a great story to tell about the chase. So with all this liquor being transported by daring young men in fast cars, it was inevitable that racing would begin.

Tracks popped up everywhere and anywhere. It was interesting so people showed up to watch and that, in turn, was interesting to promoters who began offering prize money for particular races. The problem was that many of the promoters collected gate receipts and then disappeared before the race was finished. Early racing was, apparently, an unscrupulous business.

Plus there were different rules at different tracks and even different kinds of cars all racing against each other. Lawbreaking drivers would run from the police during the week and run circles around the track on weekends.

And in the early days racetracks were rough places where, legend has it, fighting could start almost as easily as a race. Racers arrived anyway and they challenged for the money and for the glory and because they loved to race and the fans loved to watch. The story had begun.

Racing was particularly popular up and down this Whiskey Belt, which encompassed the Appalachian Mountains. But one other spot in particular began to get the attention of drivers. That was the hard-packed sands of Daytona Beach, Florida, where they drivers set records on *The Daytona Beach Course*.

### Pit Stop!

**The Daytona Beach Course** was the original stretch of Ormond Beach in Daytona where many land speed records were set. From the earliest part of the century, racers came to Daytona Beach like a racing Mecca, because at low tide it provided a long stretch of hard sand where you could go really fast.

Speed records were set in Daytona Beach early in the century and it continued to draw record chasers until 1935 when the man with the fastest car, Malcolm Campbell, went west to the salt flats of Bonneville, Utah, where he found even more room to go fast. Others soon followed.

So in 1936, the city of Daytona Beach did the one thing that government is good at—it threw money at the problem. In this particular case, by creating the *Daytona Beach and Road Course*, it worked beautifully.

### Pit Stop!

**The Daytona Beach and Road Course** was an oval racetrack (it has since been replaced) that started on Route A1A, turned left onto the hard sands of Daytona Beach, and then turned back onto Route A1A. The original length was 3.2 miles, but it was lengthened to 4.2 miles in the 1940s. It closed in 1959.

Interestingly enough, just two years earlier, a gangly tall mechanic named Bill France had arrived in Daytona Beach, after moving his family south from Maryland. France, you see, liked cars a lot.

# Bill France and the Formation of NASCAR

Big Bill France (he was 6'5" tall, thus the moniker) was the first president of NASCAR.

That's your foundation of information. Here's the back story: once upon a time—say, 1934—Bill France Sr. (there's a Jr. in this story, too) moved from Maryland to Florida to get out of the cold and when he arrived in Daytona Beach, on his way to Miami, he stopped. There was something about the place he liked. Plus, in the middle of the Great Depression, he quickly found a job fixing cars at a local dealership.

*Big Bill France, the first president of NASCAR*

*(Courtesy of BRH Racing Archives.)*

In Daytona Beach, when the first race was held on the oval in 1936, France entered and finished, according to legend, in fifth place. But the city lost $22,000 on that race, and by 1938 it needed help so France jumped in and began helping promote races at that track.

He wanted racers to receive prizes for leading the most number of laps as well as for winning the race. In the first race that France promoted, prizes included a bottle of rum, case of Pennzoil Motor Oil, a box of Have-a-Tampa cigars, and two cases of Pabst Blue Ribbon Beer.

**Awesome!**

In the first race that Bill France staged on the Daytona Beach and Road Course, France himself raced and came in second—to a cheater who illegally changed the cylinder heads on his racecar. France disqualified the cheater, Smokey Purser, but he didn't declare himself the winner. He gave the victory to the third place finisher, Lloyd Moody.

France kept promoting races until World War II intervened, when many racers went to war. France went to work in a shipyard to support the war effort. When the war ended and the soldiers came home, the auto factories kick started up again and the urge to race also started back up. France noticed. So did other race promoters in other parts of the Southeast, Northeast, and Midwest.

However, racing was a mish-mash of rules, and it seemed, in fact, that every track had its own rules. But France had a vision and had been trying with varying success to organize a sport for just stock cars. France believed that regular people would like to watch cars racing that looked just like their own. One of his organizations, the unfortunately named Stock Car Automobile Racing Society (SCARS) competed with other organizations run by other promoters.

He also approached the American Automobile Association (AAA), but that organization was only interested in high-performance Indy-type cars, not stock cars. And France was insistent that his new organization be all about stock cars. After all, he continued to insist, people would love to watch a race run by cars that look just like theirs.

So on December 14, 1947, 36 race promoters met for three days and three nights at a place called the Ebony Lounge atop the Streamline Hotel in Daytona Beach to plan a new organization. Two months later, on February 21, 1948, the National Association for Stock Car Auto Racing (NASCAR) was incorporated. France was president and majority stockholder. France's grandson, Brian France, is currently the president of NASCAR.

# Early NASCAR, Strictly Stock Division

In the first season, France had yet to exert the totalitarian control that would be his standard procedure in years to come. Instead, in that inaugural season of 1948, many racers drove modified hot rods.

It wasn't until the 1949 season that NASCAR's rules for its premier racing series called for all cars in the race to be American-made stock cars. And they could not be modified.

On June 19, 1949, on a three-quarter mile dirt track in Charlotte, North Carolina, NASCAR staged its first race with a field full of only stock cars.

It was a 150-mile race that would set the tone for the sport all the way into current-day NASCAR. The total prize money was $5,000, with $2,000 going to the first place finisher and $1,000 to the runner up. It was a huge amount of money at the time.

**Awesome!**

Nine different brands of automobiles entered the first all stock car race held by NASCAR: Buick, Cadillac, Chrysler, Ford, Hudson, Kaiser, Lincoln, Mercury, and Oldsmobile.

But the driver who finished first that day, Glenn Dunnaway, was quickly disqualified when officials discovered he had modified his rear springs so his car handled like a bootlegger's car with more traction and handling. The owner of Dunnaway's car, Hubert Westmoreland, sued NASCAR but the case was thrown out and France's totalitarian control had begun.

**Awesome!**

Richard Petty, at 11 years old, attended the first strictly stock car race with his father, the racer Lee Petty. Lee wrecked the borrowed family car of a friend halfway through the race. So Richard Petty, who went on to become the greatest NASCAR driver of all time, had to hitchhike home from that very first race.

And cheating, though far from eliminated in stock car racing, was no longer done quite as brazenly again. Close, but not quite (more in Chapter 6). In 1949, the top level of Bill France's NASCAR was called the Strictly Stock Division, and he meant it. Cars were supposed to be like those off the showroom floor.

# NASCAR Grand National Series

In 1950, the name of the premier NASCAR series was changed from the pedestrian sounding Strictly Stock Division to the more grandeur name—the NASCAR Grand National Series.

It was grand, it was national, and it was a series. There were rules, and France—who was also a car owner, ran it. He would soon be involved in the ownership of racetracks as well.

Stock cars. The entire idea was to race stock cars and, in France's vision, grow the sport. 1950 was a big year in stock car racing because that was the year that a 1.366-mile asphalt track opened in Darlington, North Carolina. A man named Harold Brasington put down the track, and it had high banks designed for some very fast racing.

Darlington. To racing fans, the track is known as "The Lady in Black" because she's a heart breaker. She's a bone breaker. Darlington. She's a pioneer. When she was built, NASCAR stepped forward and the grand dance began.

It was at its genesis, of course, a Southern sport, and tracks through-out the Southeast were the circuit. Although open-wheeled racing at Indianapolis had attracted a national following and fascination since that track opened in 1909, stock car racing was blue collar, southern, and proud—whiskey proud.

When Darlington opened in 1950, whiskey-proud had gone modern. The stars were aligning with the guidance, iron will, and energy of Bill France. And on the racetracks across the Southeast, stars were emerging.

With a new name for its premier series, and a new grand cathedral in Darlington, NASCAR was poised in 1950 to begin to fulfill Bill France's vision of bringing this specific kind of racing to the people who would relate to it the most—the working people of America who owned these kind of cars. The Grand National Series was the precursor to the hero machine that is the modern Chase for the Sprint Cup.

> ### Awesome!
>
> One of the early heroes of NASCAR was a monkey. Jocko Flocko, the monkey, rode nine races in 1953 with the legendary colorful driver, Tim Flock. In the ninth race of the publicity stunt, the monkey attacked Flock mid-race. At a pit stop, Flock then kicked the monkey out of his car. It was the end of literal monkey business in NASCAR.

Although NASCAR continues as one of the most interesting sports that America has created, the early history was particularly colorful—maybe because many of the races actually included real bootleggers such as Junior Johnson, who once, while running from the police, stopped to steal gas from a tractor but then felt guilty and left $200 behind for the tractor owner. Johnson was actually later arrested at his father's still and served 11 months in federal prison. Many years later, he was pardoned by President Ronald Reagan.

But while the characters (more in Chapter 11) were weaving their own rich history, the sport itself was evolving from its strictly stock roots into something much more complex.

Strictly stock cars, it turned out, were dangerous to race at such high speeds. So slowly through the years, NASCAR allowed for changes to the cars. On the outside, they still looked like stock cars from the showroom floor. But inside was another matter entirely.

In 1952, roll bars were added for safety. Also that year, two-way radios were first used in a race, and the first racing tires were used.

But while safety devices were added in the 1950s, cars kept

> ### Awesome!
>
> To check for tire wear, drivers used a trap door in the floorboard, which they would open in order to look at the tires. Drivers stopped to change tires if they saw the white cord of the worn tire as they were driving.

getting faster as engine development for racing took off. Meanwhile, many of the drivers were moonshiners themselves, while others were simply full-fledged members of that moonshine generation and they lived and drove like it.

These were not tame people. On the other hand, these were not dull people either. It was a crazy time in a crazy sport with a bunch of wild-eyed drivers who lived for danger. They were not the corporate spokesman type. Drivers often drove hung over, if not just plain drunk, and there are even stories of drivers actually riding with a jug in their car.

And NASCAR rules, it seems, were made to be broken, because as soon as France started enforcing a specific set of rules, most drivers began looking for advantages. It is a game that continues into current NASCAR.

But perhaps the most important factor in bringing NASCAR forward was the construction of more new, modern tracks. Besides the gem of Darlington, many of the tracks run in NASCAR in the Southeast were dirt tracks. And even the beach and road course in Daytona, although charming and fascinating, was not conducive to the kind of racing that was now becoming possible. By 1953, Bill France realized it and began to plan for something amazing—a track almost twice the size of Darlington.

# Daytona International Speedway Gets Built

In 1959, the Daytona International Speedway opened. It was a 2.5-mile, tri-oval gem with 31-degree banking in the corners. From the grandstands, an observer could see virtually the entire track.

Bill France was a dreamer. He was a doer as well, but first came the dreams. By 1953 France saw his first vision, organized stock car racing, coming true. He began to believe that a paved track in Daytona would advance the sport further. So, of course, he dreamt as big as he could—to the point that the drivers actually expressed concern before his new track even opened. Drivers, who loved speed, were worried the track might be too fast.

But France was undeterred, and after five years he found almost $2 million in necessary funding. Construction began in 1958. The track opened in February 1959 with a series of races. The final was a 500-mile race for a total prize of $60,160. It was the largest prize in racing history and it garnered NASCAR big-time attention. Even *Sports Illustrated* took note of the first Daytona 500.

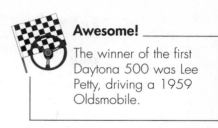

**Awesome!**

The winner of the first Daytona 500 was Lee Petty, driving a 1959 Oldsmobile.

France believed in a truly visionary way that someday the Daytona 500 would be as big as the Indianapolis 500. At the time, it seemed preposterous. Now, the Daytona 500 is arguably much more popular than the open-wheeled racing that occurs in the Indianapolis 500.

# The 1960s—A Time for Change

When the Daytona International Speedway opened in 1959, NASCAR was poised for growth. Money began to flow into the sport in ways not imagined before as the major car companies noticed a correlation between winning on Sunday and selling on Monday.

Even in the 1950s, France began migrating the sport out of the Southeast to tracks in New York and Wisconsin. During the '60s the migration continued but the base remained in the Southeast.

Change was occurring in many ways, not all of them appreciated by the czar of NASCAR, Big Bill France. For one thing, drivers were restless. Danger was increasing, money wasn't big enough, and France was holding his monopoly so close that some drivers, in order to make extra money in non-NASCAR races, had to actually change their names to participate in what was then called the outlaw circuit.

The Teamsters even tried to organize the drivers but that tough labor union was no match for France, who declared no known Teamster member can drive in a NASCAR race. Meanwhile, France was happy to team up with the Teamsters' nemesis, big automakers from Detroit. The car companies, particularly Ford, were spending millions of dollars on NASCAR racing in the mid-1960s.

## Talladega and the Driver's Revolt

By the late 1960s, France opened a new superspeedway (the name for really long tracks, see Chapters 3 and 5) in Talladega, Alabama. This 2.66-mile track had longer straightaways than Daytona and turns that banked two degrees higher than Daytona's. Talladega was fast. Before it even opened, drivers feared it was deadly fast. Testing before the first Talladega race produced numerous blown tires as the speeds seemed too much for the tires to withstand.

Drivers were worried. A new organization, the Professional Drivers Association (PDA) had recently formed with the purpose of improving conditions for drivers. Richard Petty was the president of PDA, and another famous driver, Cale Yarborough, was the vice president. The PDA actually staged a boycott of the first Grand National Race at Talladega.

France, stubborn as ever, simply ran the race with drivers from a lower level (there are levels in racing, see Chapter 3). There were no accidents and France said that this proved the track is safe. Though the dispute was quickly resolved and the star racers have since raced at Talladega, this incident continued to cement France as the supreme ruler of NASCAR.

## Aerodynamics

Automobile manufacturers had taken engine development for racing to new levels and pushed the cars to amazing speeds, but the ability to get more horsepower began to take a backseat to aerodynamics.

In 1969 and 1970, car designs appeared on the NASCAR circuit that were not like what was seen on the road. These racecars had wings, sloped noses, and sloped back ends, and though they looked very cool, they were not in synch with the original vision of strictly stock cars. Examples of these cars include the 1969 Dodge Charger Daytona, the 1970 Plymouth Superbird, and the 1969 Ford Torino Talladega. (There were street versions of all these cars built and sold to the public. NASCAR mandated that 1,000 street examples had to be built in order for a car to be eligible for competition.)

So NASCAR banned the cars. (They actually weren't banned outright but their engine size was restricted so it amounted to a ban.)

# Winston Cup, 1972–2003

From 1972 to 2003, the championship of NASCAR was known as The Winston Cup. Many NASCAR fans view this as the beginning of the modern era.

The R. J. Reynolds Tobacco Company became the major sponsor of NASCAR in 1972. For a long time, it was a perfect marriage of sport and sponsor.

Tobacco advertisements had recently been banned from television and the big company was looking for a new, legal way to market their product. NASCAR, as sort of an outlaw sport anyway with roots in bootlegging, also had roots in North Carolina, where tobacco is grown. It was a natural partnership.

**Awesome!**

Former bootlegger Junior Johnson made the first contact with R.J. Reynolds. He wanted them to sponsor his car, but the company had much bigger ideas so Johnson put them in touch with NASCAR president Bill France.

The year 1972 was a big year of change for NASCAR. The name of the premier series became the Winston Cup Grand National Series. (It was shortened to Winston Cup Series in 1986.)

But that name change signified more important changes. In addition, dirt tracks were dropped from the circuit, and Bill France's son, Bill France Jr., took the reigns of NASCAR. A new era had begun.

The Winston sponsorship brought about advancements in the sport and an influx of much-needed money. The growing power of television also caught notice, but at first only in a small way—mostly airing snippets on ABC's popular show, Wide World of Sports.

## The 1979 Daytona 500

In many important ways, America discovered stock car racing on February 18, 1979. That was the first national broadcast of an entire start-to-finish 500-mile NASCAR race. And it was one of the most exciting races ever—a pivotal moment for the sport. (On April 10, 1971 ABC Sports aired a live 100-mile Winston Cup race from Greenville-Pickens Speedway in Greenville SC, live from start to finish.)

Coincidentally, a major snowstorm had shut down almost the entire East Coast. And this was back in an era when there were only three channels on. NASCAR had a captive audience, and it delivered the kind of entertainment that America loves.

It was a chaotic crazy race that ended with a final lap showdown between drivers Donnie Allison and Cale Yarborough. As they bumped on the backstretch, with both cars literally battling to stay straight, they both eventually lost control and slammed into the wall before settling in the infield. Meanwhile Richard Petty went by them for the win. But that was just the beginning of the drama.

Suddenly Yarborough was screaming at Donnie Allison, and Bobby Allison, Donnie's brother and another driver, pulled up. Cameras rolled. Yarborough started swinging a helmet, then fists, and then Donnie Allison's fists were hitting him. It was wild. It was madness.

And America loved it. Television had discovered the passion of NASCAR.

## The Restrictor Plate for Superspeedways, 1988

NASCAR mandated the use of restrictor plates, limiting the horsepower of a car at superspeedways, in 1988. (Restrictor plates were used in cup cars as early as 1970; they made a return in 1988.)

This followed the horrifying crash at Talladega in 1987 that sent Bobby Allison's Buick LeSabre airborne towards a fence that could have easily been near spectators. (Bobby's car tore down about 100 feet of fence and sent two people to the hospital.) Fearing for the audience, with cars that were now surpassing 200 miles per hour, NASCAR slowed the cars down.

This created a completely different kind of racing, restrictor plate racing, in which teamwork is as important as anything, since, theoretically, all cars are just as fast.

## Black Sunday, 2001

On February 18, 2001, one of the most successful and popular drivers in NASCAR history, Dale Earnhardt, died when his black number 3 Chevrolet crashed into the wall on the final lap of the Daytona 500.

Earnhardt, who was called "The Intimidator" for his no-fear driving style, was an iconic figure and his passing reverberated far beyond the NASCAR world. He was a figure from popular culture, and TV news as well as magazines and newspapers took note. On its darkest day, NASCAR received its most publicity. And from that day forward, NASCAR was in the big time.

The accident, along with others in the previous year, also brought along safety changes—such as safer walls and a device to hold the head in place during accidents. (Three drivers died the year before Earnhardt. In 2000, Adam Petty died in Busch series car, Kenny Irwin died in a cup car, and Tony Roper died in a truck, all from the same type injury as Earnhardt.)

# The Nextel Cup, 2004 to 2007, and Now the Sprint Cup

In 2004, the communications company, Nextel, took over sponsorship of the premier series in NASCAR. The name was changed from Winston Cup to Nextel Cup, and Nextel paid $700 million for ten-year naming rights to the series.

Since then, Nextel was purchased by Sprint. As part of the deal, Nextel was allowed one name change for the premier series. The series is called the Sprint Cup as of the 2008 season.

NASCAR continues to be one of the fastest-growing, exciting sports in the world. The reasons are obvious to anyone who has followed the sport for any length of time.

## The Least You Need to Know

◆ Bootlegging is at the roots of NASCAR. Bootleggers bragging about their fast cars led to the first races.

◆ Bill France formed NASCAR in 1947 with 35 other men in the Ebony Lounge atop the Streamline Hotel in Daytona Beach, Florida.

◆ The modern era began in 1972 when R.J. Reynolds took over sponsorship and the name of prize for the premier series was changed to the Winston Cup.

◆ Dale Earnhardt died on Black Sunday—February 18, 2001, on the final lap of the Daytona 500.

◆ The name Winston Cup was changed to Nextel Cup starting in the 2004 season.

◆ The name Nextel Cup will be changed to Sprint Cup starting for the 2008 season and beyond.

# Chapter 3

# Turn Left—NASCAR Basics

## In This Chapter

- ◆ A look at the basic rules of a race
- ◆ The flags of NASCAR
- ◆ An explanation of the various levels in NASCAR

Cars start at the start/finish line and they subsequently finish (if they finish) at the start/finish line. And no, this does not mean that the space/time continuum has somehow warped. It just means that the cars go in a circle when they race. And in order to go in a circle (well, an oval), they have to turn in one particular direction over and over again. These cars turn left.

This is a chapter about the basics of NASCAR racing. It will also give a primer on the various-sized tracks, as well as a discussion of pit stops and the flags of the road. It will also include information on how NASCAR has levels and explain that Sprint Cup racing is the highest level.

# A NASCAR Primer

◆ The top level of NASCAR racing is Sprint Cup racing. The next levels down are the Busch Series and the Craftsman Truck Series.

◆ Forty-three cars start every Sprint Cup race and every Busch race.

◆ Thirty-six trucks start every Craftsman Truck race.

◆ Races are held on different-size and -shape tracks, each with distinct characteristics.

◆ Racing is expensive, which explains the corporate logos.

◆ A pit stop is where a car gets gas, new tires, general repairs and adjustments in seconds.

◆ Safety is a primary concern.

# Basic Rules of a Race

Cars line up by twos and follow a pace car until the start of the race. The race starts at the start/finish line.

When there is an accident, and the yellow caution flag is out, cars must slow down and maintain their position in the race behind the pace car, unless they happen to be the *lucky dog*.

**Pit Stop!**

The **lucky dog** is the car one lap down that is the closest to the lead lap when the caution flag comes out. That car automatically gets the lap back unless it is during the final ten laps of the race.

When the green flag is out, cars can race. The first car to finish wins the race.

# Different-Size Tracks

Variety is the spice of NASCAR. In Sprint Cup racing, drivers are subjected to some wildly different conditions—from the 2.66-mile Talladega Superspeedway to the 0.533 high-banked cereal bowl that is Bristol Motor Speedway.

Different-size tracks make for different kinds of racing. For more on the tracks of the Sprint Cup, see Chapter 5.

# Pit Stops

Races are long and cars need to be worked on sometimes. Just like you, they need gas and sometimes they need tires. Well, they wear out their tires a lot faster than you wear out yours.

*(Courtesy of Bryan Haltman.)*

*A pit stop. These guys are a little faster than your local mechanic.*

When cars stop to get worked on, they stop in a place called pit row. The pit is simply the place where the car gets worked on. What happens in pit row can determine the outcome of a race. For more on pit stops, see Chapter 9.

# Safety and Flags

Racing is dangerous but here's the thing everyone involved understands:

Crashes happen.

Therefore changes have been made to the racecars (see Chapter 6) and the tracks (see Chapter 5) to improve safety. And yet, the oldest system of all is still the one that makes it all work—flags.

NASCAR utilizes flags to alert drivers to what is going on in the race. Flags alert drivers to a number of things. Here are the flags of a NASCAR race:

| | |
|---|---|
| Green | Go racing. This signals restarts after a caution. |
| Yellow | Slow down. Caution. The track is not clear. Hold your position in the race behind the pace car. |
| Red | The track is unsafe. Stop. |
| White | One lap left. |
| Checkered | The race is over. |
| Black | Usually aimed at a particular car. It means come into the pits. There is a mechanical problem, or you have broken a rule. |
| Black with white cross | You will not be scored until you come into the pits. Cars that ignore the black are shown this. |
| Blue with yellow stripe | Aimed at a particular car. Watch out behind. A faster car is approaching. |
| Yellow with red vertical stripes | Only used on corners in road courses to signify slippery or dangerous conditions. |

# More Than One Level of Racing

The National Association for Stock Car Automobile Racing (NASCAR) is an organization that oversees many types and levels of racing. Currently, NASCAR oversees three national divisions:

- ◆ Sprint Cup Series
- ◆ Busch Series
- ◆ Craftsman Truck Series

The premier league in NASCAR—the one with the superstar drivers in the Sunday televised races—is Sprint Cup Racing. More on that later.

NASCAR was born in 1947 as a means to organize the sport so that the rules at various tracks would be the same. (See Chapter 2.) As the organization has grown and evolved, NASCAR has overseen numerous leagues through the years. There were other major divisions in the past including, believe it or not, a Convertible Division.

The Convertible Division ran in the late 1950s as a way to showcase the drivers. Richard Petty, the greatest driver in history, made his debut driving convertibles. And the very first race held at the Daytona International Speedway was a 100-mile convertible race.

The amazing thing about the Convertible Division was that sometimes the convertibles would race against hardtop cars and sometimes they could transform. These were called *zipper top cars.*

 **Pit Stop!**

**Zipper top cars** were convertibles that could easily be converted into hardtop stock cars. There was no zipper. The top was bolted on.

Another early division, tried by NASCAR in 1952, was the Speedway Division, which featured Indy style cars. It didn't survive.

Racing is a wide open field attracting all kinds of racing, and evolution has always been inevitable. Even the premier league itself has had five names—Strictly Stock Car Division, Grand National Series, Winston

Cup, Nextel Cup, and now Sprint Cup—since 1947. (For more, see Chapter 2).

Although Sprint Cup racing is the racing that garners all the publicity, NASCAR has always overseen more than just one division.

# The Top Three Series

The relationship between the three top series …

◆ Sprint Cup Series

◆ Busch Series

◆ Craftsman Truck Series

… is something like that of major league and minor league baseball. The Sprint Cup Series is the top series (major league), the Busch Series is the second-tier series (AAA using the baseball analogy), and the Craftsman Truck Series is the third tier (AA). Yet some drivers drive in all three series. This is because owners (see Chapters 1 and 10) often participate in all three series. And so the baseball analogy is not exactly correct, but it is a helpful guide to understanding the relationship between the three series.

The big difference between this system and that used by baseball is that sometimes crewmembers or drivers participate in more than one of the series.

It's a feeder system—for drivers and for the pit crew. And it's a practice system as well, since often all three events are held on the same track on the same weekend. Therefore, a driver might drive in the Busch series on Saturday to get a sense of how the track will handle on Sunday. Plus, keep in mind that drivers are independent contractors, able, essentially, to drive for whomever they want.

If a cup driver chooses to drive in the other series, he may be doing so for practice. After all, the more times you go around the track, the more you get a feel for how it drives. It's like anything in life. Repetition makes you better. You know, practice makes … well, nobody's perfect. That's why they practice.

There are two other reasons why a driver might drive in more than one series:

◆ It's fun to drive.

◆ There is money to be won.

## Craftsmen Truck Series

The first step into the big time is in a truck. It's also sometimes the last step down. Often, young drivers are competing with veteran cup drivers and even with some current cup drivers just looking for extra fun or money.

Truck racing is relatively new in NASCAR. The original series, called the Supertruck Series, started in 1995. It took on the name Craftsman Truck Series in 1996.

The truck season is 25 races long and many, though not all, of the truck races are held on the same weekends and at the same tracks as the Sprint Cup races. In that case, Craftsman Truck races are held on Fridays. (Some races are held on Saturdays at different non-cup tracks.)

 **Awesome!**

The 2006 Craftsman Truck champion, Todd Bodine, drove full seasons in Winston Cup (now Sprint Cup) racing in 2001 and 2003.

Truck racing is very different than stock car racing but the skills are somewhat transferable. However, the differences are dramatic, including, obviously, the design of the vehicle. But it goes beyond that to include a shorter schedule and an operating budget that is miniscule compared to a Sprint Cup car.

But fans agree that trucks produce an exciting brand of side-by-side racing with perhaps the most interesting mix of drivers of any of the top three series.

*(Courtesy of Bryan Hallman.)*

*Craftsman Truck Racing.*

## Busch Series/New Sponsor TBA

This minor league series is being renamed for the 2008 season. This series, which features stock cars very similar to those that run in Sprint Cup racing, runs 35 races in its season.

And again, calling this a minor league is somewhat of a misnomer. Busch racing is just shorter, different kind of racing that serves as a feeder system for Sprint Cup racing.

**Pit Stop!**

**Buschwhackers** is a term for Sprint Cup drivers who also drive in the Busch series.

But many cup drivers like to drive in Busch races to get a feel for the track for the upcoming Sunday cup race as well as to have the fun of competing. Some of the most exciting racing occurs on Saturdays in Busch racing when the young guns of Busch racing compete with the *Buschwhackers*.

These are typically shorter races than Sprint Cup races and the talent level is wide enough that it can sometimes make for exciting finishes with drivers charging through the field in the final laps to challenge for a lead. Otherwise, the racing is very similar because the cars are so similar and often the drivers are the same. Or the pit crew is the same. Or the owners are the same.

It's the mixture of youth and experience that makes Busch racing different than Sprint Cup racing, and money plays a large part in the difference. The cost of a Busch car is about half that of a cup car. Reasons for this include shorter races and lower overhead.

Anheuser-Busch is relinquishing sponsorship of the series after the 2007 season. The brewing giant owned the series for 26 years and paid in recent years an estimated $15 million per year for the rights.

The new sponsor, an unknown corporation as of press time, is expected to pay much more for naming rights to the growing series.

## Sprint Cup Racing

Sprint Cup racing is the mountaintop.

When you think of NASCAR as *something*, when you see the commercials, when you buy the gear, the version you are thinking of is Sprint Cup racing. Although Busch and cup racing are similar:

◆ Cup cars have a little more horsepower than Busch cars.

◆ Cup cars have a five-inch longer front-to-rear wheel base.

◆ Cup cars have a shorter rear spoiler.

Quite simply, Sprint Cup racing is where legends are made. The great stories are cup stories because that kind of racing has the best cars, the best owners, the best drivers, and the best pit crews. It's where great minds, incredible motivation, and spectacular talent are on display for the nation to watch.

# Local NASCAR

NASCAR is a big organization that runs deeper than the three major series. Below the three major divisions are regional series sanctioned by NASCAR. Through the years there have been many smaller and regional series with different sponsors and the names sometimes change year to year.

And, in fact, NASCAR actually also sanctions races involving modified cars, which are open-wheeled vehicles that are not even stock cars.

Plus, NASCAR is not the only organization to sanction stock car races. But most of the talent that rises into the top levels of NASCAR comes from NASCAR-sanctioned lower levels. Nevertheless, you can most likely find exciting racing happening somewhere near you.

## NASCAR Grand National Division—Busch East Series; West Series

Each coast has its own series operating under identical rules, which are similar to the rules of Busch Series racing.

What is now called the Grand National Division (not to be confused with one of the original name of Sprint Cup Racing—see Chapter 2) is a feeder division into the top level of racing. If you make it to this series, people are noticing you.

The West Series is much older than the Busch East Series. The West Series began in 1953, whereas the Busch East Series (formerly known as the Busch North Series) began in 1987.

## Whelen All-American Series

NASCAR sanctions a grassroots-racing program that is held at small tracks across the country.

Typically run at short tracks, these races are the beginning, local feeder series where NASCAR goes to find its *development drivers*.

**Pit Stop!**

**Development driver** is the name for a driver who is in the system and trying to earn the right to drive a cup car.

Peyton Sellers of Danville, Virginia, is an example of a development driver. In 2005, at the age of 21, Sellers was the champion of a track in South Boston, Virginia.

Through a complicated system of scoring that pits drivers at different tracks against each other, Sellers was national champion (the Whelen All-American series was previously called the Dodge Weekly Series) in 2005. At that point, he was picked up by Richard Childress Racing to race in the Busch East Series. He has since driven in the Busch Series and may be on his way to driving a cup car. In other words, he is being developed. Racers such as Sellers can be found at tracks across the country.

This series is sponsored by the Connecticut-based Whelen Engineering, a leading manufacturer of automotive, aviation, industrial, and public emergency lighting systems.

## Whelen Modified

Throughout its history, NASCAR has sanctioned races for modified stock cars. Modified cars are simply stock cars that have been modified to perform on short tracks. If you look closely, you might be able to make out the original make of the car.

For some reason, modified cars have been historically more popular in the Northeast than in other parts of the country. There are currently two divisions—the Whelen Modified Division, based at tracks in the Northeast, and the Whelen Southern Modified Division, based in the South.

## The Least You Need to Know

- Races are run on different-size tracks with different characteristics.
- Pit stops are where cars get gas and new tires.
- Flags are used to communicate to drivers. Green means go. Yellow means caution. Checkered means the race is over.
- Sprint Cup racing is the top level of racing.
- You can find a racetrack near you.

# Chapter 4

# The Sprint Cup Season

## In This Chapter

- How often are the races?
- How do you keep score?
- Who qualifies for a race?
- How do you win the championship?

"Gentleman, start your engines."

Beginning in the middle of February, those magical words signal the start of 36 NASCAR Sprint Cup races held almost once a week at a different racetrack all across America.

But the individual races themselves are part of something bigger—much bigger. The Sprint Cup race season is 10 months long, the longest season in professional sports. It is grueling, dramatic, and unpredictable. There are even playoffs—called the Chase for the Sprint Cup—and at the end a champion is crowned.

Yes, the top level of racing, just like other sports, has a season and it crowns a champion. But because of the nature of NASCAR, in which 43 cars enter every race, the rules are a little bit different. Some would even say contrived.

This is a chapter about the season itself, and how a Sprint Cup champion is crowned.

# A New Track A Week ...

Almost every week for ten months, NASCAR roars. It's like a traveling circus coming to a town near you, only the acts on display are much more exciting than anything a master of ceremonies could ever imagine.

Speed is coming to your town, or at least to 22 different race tracks all over the United States. In fact, there are many different kinds of racetracks, as you will learn in Chapter 5.

During the Cup season, drivers are tested on small and large tracks in races that vary from 300 to 600 miles. Yes, there is a season.

**Awesome!**

Pre-race ceremonies always include a military flyover, as well as a prayer and the National Anthem.

There is, in fact, a schedule that begins in the middle of February on the Superspeedway in Daytona and runs until November in Homestead, Florida.

Between the first race in Daytona and the final race in Homestead, NASCAR criss-crosses the country. It's a grueling, barnstorming tour of America. And while each race is surely an endurance test in itself, the bigger marathon of an almost never-ending season is truly the big test—and it is one that crowns the champion. Driver, crew, and equipment are pushed to the limit for ten long months.

It's a sprint. It's also a marathon. But to understand NASCAR is to understand that it is about change and evolution and variables. Like many things, the schedule has changed through the years and it is always possible for it to change again, even year to year.

So although the Cup season starts with the Daytona 500, it hasn't always been a 36-race season. In fact, it hasn't always been called the Sprint Cup either (see Chapter 2).

And as new racetracks have been built, races have moved. And that trend may continue as NASCAR continues to extend its reach from its roots in the Southeast to all parts of the country.

Generally, the season progresses about the same way every year although some races are sometimes flip-flopped. Sometimes, even during the season, a new sponsor may be added and the name of a race could change.

**Awesome!** _____

Beyond the 36 races that count for points toward the Sprint Cup, NASCAR runs three non-point events that also draw all the best drivers. These non-point races are the Budweiser Shootout, the Gatorade Duel, and the Sprint All-Star Challenge.

# The Points System

Wait a minute. Points?

Yes, points. Racing isn't like other sports where teams compete directly against each other. Instead, 43 drivers compete to win each race and points are given out for finishing from 1st to 43rd.

In fact, NASCAR officials, through the years, developed a points system based on victories as well as leading for a lap or leading the most laps in a race. The system has changed and may continue to change.

For 2007, the rules were:

◆ Race winners receive 185 points.

◆ Leading for at least one lap earns 5 points

◆ Leading for the most laps earns 5 points

Thus, a winner can receive a maximum of 195 points.

The second place finisher receives 170 points plus bonus points for leading a lap or leading the most laps. Plus, NASCAR is strictly controlled and if a racer is caught cheating, he may be penalized points.

Here is the 2007 scoring system for all finishers.

## 2007 Nextel Cup Scoring System

| FINISH | POINTS | FINISH | POINTS | FINISH | POINTS |
|--------|--------|--------|--------|--------|--------|
| 1 | 185 | 16 | 115 | 30 | 73 |
| 2 | 170 | 17 | 112 | 31 | 70 |
| 3 | 165 | 18 | 109 | 32 | 67 |
| 4 | 160 | 19 | 106 | 33 | 64 |
| 5 | 155 | 20 | 103 | 34 | 61 |
| 6 | 150 | 21 | 100 | 35 | 58 |
| 7 | 146 | 22 | 97 | 36 | 55 |
| 8 | 142 | 23 | 94 | 37 | 52 |
| 9 | 138 | 24 | 91 | 38 | 49 |
| 10 | 134 | 25 | 88 | 39 | 46 |
| 11 | 130 | 26 | 85 | 40 | 43 |
| 12 | 127 | 27 | 82 | 41 | 40 |
| 13 | 124 | 28 | 79 | 42 | 37 |
| 14 | 121 | 29 | 76 | 43 | 34 |
| 15 | 118 | | | | |

First place is not always 195 points. It is only 195 points if the winner leads the most laps, which is not always the case. In some races, the second place finisher, for example, may lead the most laps. In that case, the winner would earn 190 points (185 + 5 extra for leading one race) and the second place driver would earn 180 points (170 + 5 for leading a lap + 5 more for leading the most.

# Who Qualifies?

But before a team has a chance at points, it has to first qualify for the race by doing a two-lap time trial. Each lap is timed and the fastest lap counts. But a funny thing happened on the way to qualifying. Some teams have already made it.

# Thirty-five Cars Are in on Owner Points

Thirty-five teams have already made it based upon *owner points*.

> **Pit Stop!**
>
> All teams acquire **owner points.** Each car has an owner. Even if there is a different driver, the car accumulates owner points. Just by being inspected and attempting to qualify, a team gets some owner points. Owners are rewarded for showing up. The fastest team in a timed lap (44th place) not to qualify receives 31 points. Each subsequent nonqualifier would receive 3 points less, down to a minimum of 1 point. (Oddly, only owners receive these points. Drivers must actually race to get points toward the Cup.)

That's right, 35 of the 43 spots are locked up before time trials. In the 2007 season:

◆ The top 35 teams in owner points from the 2006 season qualified for the first five races.

◆ After the first five races, the top 35 teams in 2007 owner points qualify for each subsequent race.

Of course, if you qualified for all of the first five races, there's a good chance your team is in the top owner points going forward. It's a distinct advantage that is often self-perpetuating.

One reason for owner points is to ensure that the sponsors, who pay big money to support these teams, have a legitimate chance to have their logos seen in the race. NASCAR needs money and sponsors give money. The logic is actually as simple as 1+1.

So the top 35 in owner points get in. Simple enough, right? Well, wait—most owners own more than one car. But you know what? It doesn't matter.

Even though they are called owner points—each car (actually, not the specific car—because owners have backups—but rather the number of the car) qualifies for points through the season.

Each car gets points. Despite the name—owner points—the owner cannot add his points together from his various cars. Yes, welcome to NASCAR logic. Yet, sometimes things are actually logical.

## Seven Cars Race Their Way In

All cars undergo time trials. Those that are qualified are racing to see where they are positioned at the start of the race. The fastest car gets the *pole position*.

But more than 43 cars show up. So 35 are in and the rest are racing for one of the few spots remaining.

### Pit Stop!

**Pole position** is the position closest to the inside at the front of the line at the start of the race. It is the optimal position to start from, and is awarded to the fastest qualifying driver.

Getting in—except at the Daytona 500, which has a special qualifying system (see below) is simply a matter of having one of the seven fastest time trials (from a car not already qualified) in a two-lap test. The difference between getting in and not getting in, even in a five-mile test at a Superspeedway such as Daytona, is fractions of a second.

## One Car Gets in as a Past Champions Provisional

Sometimes NASCAR is a touch sentimental—as well as always full of great business sense.

Each year, a champion is crowned. And those champions are, by the nature of their championship, fan favorites. So NASCAR allows a past champion who doesn't qualify by other means (owner points or by speed) to qualify for a race by the nature of their previous accomplishments. This is called a Past Champions Provisional.

If more than one past champion doesn't qualify, the provisional goes to the most recent past champion. If no provisional is used, the final spot goes to the eighth fastest qualifying time.

It used to be that a champion could use the provisional as many times as they want, but in 2007 rules were changed, limiting any past champion to six uses of the provisional in the season.

This rule can be especially helpful to someone like Dale Jarrett in 2007, the 1999 champion who switched teams in 2007 to the brand new Toyota team of Michael Waltrip Racing. The team, being new, had zero owner points going into 2007. And so the provisional was a guaranteed way in, just in case he didn't qualify for the early races.

**Awesome!**

The provisional rule was created after racing legend Richard Petty failed to qualify for the spring 1989 race at Richmond. It took effect in 1991. Petty was only one to use it that first year. He used it three times.

# Speedweeks At Daytona

It all starts in Daytona in February.

Daytona is exaggerated, bigger than life. Of course, all of NASCAR is exaggerated but when the first race at Daytona rolls around, the anticipation is enormous. After an off-season of too much talking and rumors, by the time the biggest week in racing rolls around, everyone is excited for more roar and less talk.

Speedweeks is more than a chunk of time in Daytona. It is a state of mind. It's a carnival and more—a week of constant racing, qualifying, and testing, and then it culminates in the biggest race in the world—the Daytona 500.

It all starts one week before the Daytona 500.

## The Budweiser Shootout

Held eight days before the Daytona 500, this short race (70 laps) is in many ways the opening of the season for NASCAR. Like a lot in NASCAR, the rules and even the name for this all-star event have changed through the years. It was formerly known as the Busch Clash and the Bud Shootout.

And though results from the race don't count toward the Nextel Cup, there is a lot of money to be won. In 2007, winner Tony Stewart earned $215,000 for his victory.

**Awesome!** _____

Budweiser Shootout entries are required to have a Budweiser logo. Cars owned by Richard Petty never enter the Budweiser Shootout (or its previous incarnations) because Petty once promised his mother that he would never have alcohol logos on his cars.

Among the rules in 2007:

◆ Twenty-one racers. All drivers who won pole positions in the 2006 season are eligible, as well as past Budweiser Shootout champions.

◆ Racers race 20 laps with a mandatory pit stop and then they race 50 laps.

The less crowded field and the shorter race always makes for an interesting start to the year. And racers use information gathered in the Budweiser Shootout to make adjustments for the big race—the Daytona 500.

## Qualifying for the Daytona 500

The day after the Budweiser Shootout, and exactly one week before the biggest race of the year, racers take to the track one by one for a qualifying lap.

The two fastest times get the pole position and the outside pole.

But the next step toward qualifying for the Daytona 500—for those not qualified by owner points—are two races held on Thursday before the big race. These 150-mile races are called the Gatorade Duels.

All racers who entered time trials are entered in the Gatorade Duels. Half are entered in the first race and half are entered in the second. The fastest racer in each Gatorade Duel that is not already entered in the Daytona 500 gets in.

So that gets to 37.

And then—going back to the time trial—the next five fastest times by racers outside of the previously qualified 35 qualify based on their time trial.

So that gets to 42.

Finally, the Past Champions provisional gets the field to 43. Unless, of course, the provisional is not needed. Then, the sixth fastest time from time trials not to previously qualify is in the Daytona 500.

Simple, right?

Would you like an aspirin?

## The Daytona 500

Unlike most other sports, the biggest event of the year in NASCAR is the first.

The Daytona 500—sometimes referred to as The Great American Race—has the prestige and the history and it is the race drivers most covet winning. Daytona is steeped in lore.

The Sprint Cup champion isn't crowned until 10 months later. Along the way, there is a lot of racing and even an all-star game of sorts.

# The Sprint All-Star Challenge

In May, a nonpoints event is held at Lowe's Motor Speedway in Charlotte, N.C.

Eligible racers include:

◆ Drivers who won a race in the current year or the preceding year.

◆ Cup champions of the past ten years.

◆ Winners of the All-Star Challenge in the past ten years.

◆ The first and second place drivers of the Sprint Open, a race held for nonqualified drivers just before the All-Star Challenge.

◆ One driver voted in by the fans.

The race is 80 laps divided into four segments of 20 laps. The prize is $1 million.

# The Chase for The Sprint Cup

Think of playoffs.

Except that these are sort of odd playoffs with the nonplayoff teams actually getting to play—except they don't. You follow? (Has NASCAR logic been mentioned before? Sorry.)

Anyway, after the first 26 races of the year, the top 12 racers in terms of points are entered in the Chase for the Sprint Cup for the final ten races of the year. These last ten races are the playoffs.

Here's the weird thing though. Thirty-one other cars also race in those races. All cars can win each race and the accompanying prize money. But only the 12 top racers from the first 26 races get points toward the Cup championship.

*Jimmie Johnson, 2006*
*Nextel Cup champion, hoists*
*the cup.*

*(Courtesy of Mark Hawkins.)*

At the beginning of the Chase (the last ten races) the top 12 drivers' points are set to 5000, with 10 extra points added for each victory in the first 26 races. Scoring remains the same as in the first 26 races. The driver of the top 12 with the most points at the end of the season wins the Sprint Cup championship.

## The Least You Need to Know

- From February to November, there is almost one race a week.
- Forty-three cars enter every race.
- Thirty five teams automatically qualify for every race.
- The Daytona 500 is the most important race of the year.
- The last ten races of the year are called The Chase for the Sprint Cup.
- Twelve racers qualify for The Chase.

# Chapter 5

# The Tracks of NASCAR's Sprint Cup

## In This Chapter

- ◆ A quick explanation of the differences in tracks
- ◆ Sprint Cup tracks from A to Z
- ◆ Safety at the track

The Sprint Cup season barnstorms across America from February to November, taking its action from small bang-'em-up tracks to big superspeedways and a lot of other kinds of tracks as well.

It is, in fact, a season that has evolved through the years as NASCAR has grown and extended its reach far beyond its southeastern roots. The tracks of NASCAR are a potpourri of possibilities and a showcase of American ingenuity through the years.

This is a chapter about the tracks of NASCAR. It will give an overview on the difference between tracks, describe all 22 tracks on the Sprint Cup circuit, and talk about safety.

# Types of Tracks

Some tracks are so long and fast that they are called superspeedways. The term is used in lots of different ways but it originally meant any track more than a mile long. Now, some say that there are only two superspeedways—Daytona and Talladega—because these are the only two tracks that require the restrictor plate.

Some tracks are short and crazy, harkening back to the wild roots of NASCAR. And some tracks are intermediate and modern. Plus, don't forget the road courses, which actually make drivers make some right turns.

So many things can make a difference at a track. The length is just one. Some tracks are high banked and some are flat. Some are bumpy and some are smooth. Tracks are new and old as well, creating completely different conditions as they age and accumulate rubber on the track.

NASCAR continues to evolve so new tracks get added and old tracks get subtracted, and sometimes tracks are repaved and even reconfigured. Here, then, are NASCAR tracks A to Z.

# Tracks from A to Z

**Atlanta Motor Speedway**
Hampton, Georgia
Distance 1.54 miles
Layout: Quad-oval
Seating capacity: 124,000
2007 Races: March 18, Kobalt Tools 500
         October 28, Georgia 500

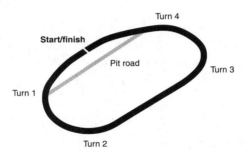

HOT TICKET: Atlanta Motor Speedway is NASCAR's fastest track. There are 24 degrees of banking in the corners and cars just fly around the asphalt. Cars run both high and low on this track, which creates some incredible side-by-side racing.

This track, which is owned by O. Bruton Smith, was completely renovated in 1997. In the renovation, the front stretch and backstretch were swapped, and the quad-oval was added. The renovation brought the track extra speed.

One characteristic of Atlanta is that engines can be tested as cars run for such a long time at such high RPMs.

**Bristol Motor Speedway**
Bristol, Tennessee
Distance: 0.533 miles
Layout: Oval
Seating Capacity: 160,000
2007 Races: March 25, Food City 500
　　　　　　　August 25, Sharpie 500

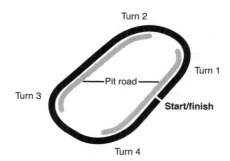

HOT TICKET: Bristol Motor Speedway is NASCAR's wildest track—famous for tempers and crashes. This small half-mile cereal bowl, paved in concrete, with the highest banking of any track—36 degrees—creates fast, bunched–up, intense racing, testing the concentration of all drivers.

Bristol is known for hardly letting any cars survive unscathed. And it's this type of testy, bumping driving that the fans love but that causes drivers to sometimes lose their tempers.

Tucked in the Appalachian Mountains of Eastern Tennessee, this speedway features a night race in August that many say is the highlight of the NASCAR season.

**California Speedway**
Fontana, California
Distance: 2 miles
Layout: D-shaped oval
Seating capacity: 92,000
2007 Races: February 25, Auto Club 500
            September 2, Nextel Cup 500

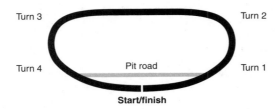

HOT TICKET: California Speedway is a two-mile asphalt oval with a smooth, fairly flat course and only 14-degree banking in the corners. This race is compelling because different strategies have been used to win—including fuel mileage and pit strategies.

This speedway is in an old industrial park 45 miles from Los Angeles, on the site of the old Kaiser Steel Mill, which was where the final scenes of the first Terminator movie were filmed.

The track is reasonably smooth and is not as hard on tires as some other tracks.

**Chicagoland Speedway**
Joliet, Illinois
Distance: 1.5 miles
Layout: D-shaped oval
Seating Capacity: 75,000
2007 Race: July 15, USG Sheetrock 400

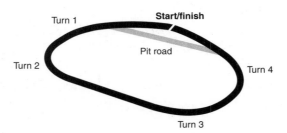

HOT TICKET: Chicagoland Speedway is a new track, having opened in 2001. This 1.5-mile track is one of the "cookie cutter" tracks that have sprung up in recent years—meaning that these tracks look similar. Chicagoland's relatively new surface is beginning to show some racing grooves, leading to some pretty good racing.

This speedway, about an hour south of Chicago, is host to a July race and in midsummer the track becomes very hot and slick. The 18-degree banked turns are just starting to develop second grooves but the racing should improve with each subsequent race.

Because of the smooth asphalt surface, tires should last on this track and, therefore, tire strategy often is critical.

**Darlington Raceway**
Darlington, South Carolina
Distance: 1.366 miles
Layout: Egg-shaped oval
Seating Capacity: 63,000
2007 Race: May 12, Dodge Avenger 500

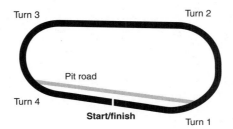

HOT TICKET: Darlington Raceway, opened in 1950, is a narrow egg-shaped oval steeped in NASCAR history as the first paved speedway of NASCAR. One end has tighter corners than the other end and this makes for tight, wall-scraping action. In fact, cars bump their right side against the wall so much that a right-side mark in the race is called a "Darlington Stripe."

Banking is 23 degrees and 25 degrees and the track is so tough that it earned the nickname "The Lady in Black" for its ability to break hearts. The tight corners were made to accommodate a minnow pond that the developer, Harold Brasington, promised would not be disturbed.

Darlington has a rough asphalt surface that eats tires.

**Daytona International Speedway**
Daytona Beach, Florida
Distance: 2.5 miles
Layout: Tri-oval
Seating capacity: 168,000
2007 Races: February 18, Daytona 500
                    July 7, Pepsi 400

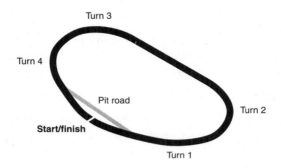

HOT TICKET: Daytona International Speedway is the most famous track of NASCAR and it hosts NASCAR's premier event, the Daytona 500. This 2.5-mile asphalt superspeedway with 31-degree banked corners is one of two tracks (Talladega) that require restrictor plates that limit the horsepower, and thus the speed, of cars.

Built in 1959 to replace a beach and road course, this track was the brainchild of Bill France Sr., the founder of NASCAR. Daytona has been host to great drama and wild finishes, and it has also been the site of great tragedy, including the 2001 death of NASCAR great Dale Earnhardt.

Strategy in restrictor-plate racing involves drafting, which means teaming up with another driver.

**Dover International Speedway**
Dover, Delaware
Distance: 1 mile
Layout: Oval
Seating Capacity: 140,000
2007 Race: June 3, Autism Speaks 400
                    September 23, Dover 400

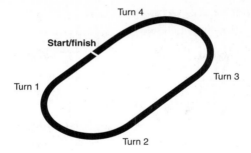

HOT TICKET: Dover International Speedway is a 1-mile concrete track with 24-degree banking. It is nicknamed "The Monster Mile" because it is such a difficult track. In fact, races here have recently been reduced from 500 miles to 400 because 500 miles wore drivers out.

Furious action is common at Dover and the race evolves as tires begin to wear out and drivers fight to find a groove that works for them. It is a tough course that makes passing difficult and time consuming as it could take a turn and a straightaway to get past even with the best strategy.

Dover's pit area is small and treacherous.

**Homestead-Miami Speedway**
Homestead, Florida
Distance: 1.5 miles
Layout: Oval
Seating Capacity: 65,000
2007 Race: November 18, Ford 400

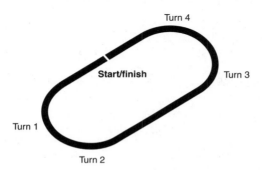

HOT TICKET: Homestead-Miami Speedway is home to the final race of the Sprint Cup season. It is, in fact, home to the final race of the Busch season and the Craftsman Truck season as well—making for a great championship weekend.

Homestead used to be a flat oval but a redesign means it now features progressive banking on an asphalt track that goes from 18 degrees to 20 degrees. The variable banking system has helped racing at this track but the multi-groove system is still a work in progress.

The best part about Homestead is its position on the schedule because if the cup chase is close, this race decides everything.

**Indianapolis Motor Speedway**
Indianapolis, Indiana
Distance: 2.5 miles
Layout: Four-cornered oval
Seating Capacity: 250,000
2007 Race: July 29, Allstate 400 at the Brickyard

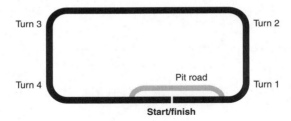

HOT TICKET: Indianapolis Motor Speedway is the historic home to another kind of automobile racing—Indy racing and the Indianapolis 500. NASCAR started visiting in 1994, and each year the Brickyard is transformed into a stock car heaven.

This distinct, four-corned oval features almost flat 9-degree banking that makes the turns on the asphalt fast and difficult. Teams face a challenge setting up their car to run on long straightaways and then to cut quickly into the four sharp corners.

Indianapolis is the oldest racetrack in the country. It was built in 1909 as an automobile proving ground.

**Infineon Raceway**
Sonoma, California
Distance: 1.99 miles
Layout: 10-turn road course
Seating Capacity: 35,000
2007 Race: June 24, Toyota/Save Mart 350

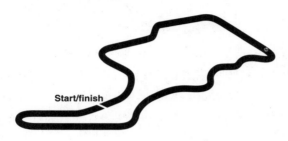

HOT TICKET: Infineon Raceway, formerly known as Sears Point, is one of only two road courses (Watkins Glen) on the Sprint Cup Circuit. Infineon is a 10-turn road course in California's wine country with changing elevations and many turns. This asphalt course is very different than anything else on the NASCAR circuit.

Drivers have to negotiate their way though tight quarters and all restarts are single file, so passing is difficult. The techniques used to drive this are very different than those used in an oval.

The scenery of the area is spectacular but the racing can take a while to develop because of the challenges of passing.

**Kansas Speedway**
Kansas City, Kansas
Distance: 1.5 miles
Layout: Tri-Oval
Seating Capacity: 81,687
2007 Race: September 30, Kansas 400

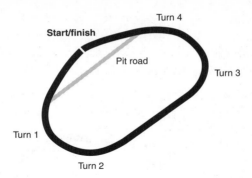

HOT TICKET: Kansas Speedway, with its 15-degree banking, is a new track, having opened in 2001. This 1.5-mile track is one of the "cookie cutter" tracks that have sprung up in recent years—meaning that these tracks look similar. Kansas Speedway's relatively new asphalt surface is beginning to show some racing grooves, leading to some pretty good racing.

This speedway is special because it is located in a big city. The racing here has already become an exciting brand with a fast track and developing grooves on the corners.

Kansas often gets long green-flag runs, which can test engines.

**Las Vegas Motor Speedway**
Las Vegas, Nevada
Distance: 1.5 miles
Layout: Oval
Seating capacity: 142,000
2007 Race: March 11, UAW-Daimler Chrysler 400

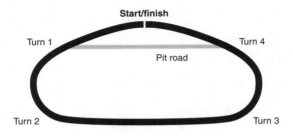

HOT TICKET: Las Vegas Motor Speedway is a fast track that changed in 2007 to make 12-degree banking in the corners into 20-degree banking. But it is still a 1.5-mile oval from the cookie cutter mold of tracks like Chicagoland and Kansas.

NASCAR in Vegas is a perfect marriage of an event and a location and so NASCAR comes here in the spring to put on a show. The new track is slick and some drivers actually thought it was too fast but they adjusted nicely to the faster corners.

**Lowe's Motor Speedway**
Concord, North Carolina
Distance: 1.5 miles
Layout: Quad-oval
Seating Capacity: 165,000
2007 Races: May 19, Nextel All-Star Challenge
                May 27, Coca-Cola 600
                October 13, Bank of America 500

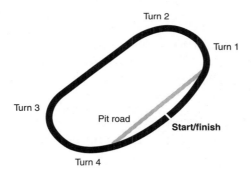

HOT TICKET: Lowe's Motor Speedway is like the home track for most NASCAR drivers, since most teams are based near this track. This track has new asphalt and 24-degree banking. In NASCAR circles, it is simply known as "Charlotte."

Speedway President H.A. "Humpy" Wheeler has created a fun atmosphere at Lowe's with plenty of entertainment besides the first-rate racing that is always available here.

The quad-oval track, with small turns on the front stretch, sends drivers flying within inches of the wall at each turn and gives interesting opportunities for passing.

**Martinsville Speedway**
Martinsville, Virginia
Distance: 0.526 miles
Layout: Oval
Seating Capacity: 65,500
2007 Races: April 1, Goody's Cool Orange 500
October 21, Subway 500

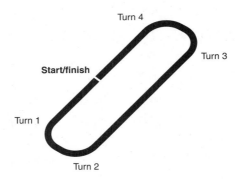

HOT TICKET: Martinsville Speedway, built in 1947, was once a dirt track in NASCAR's early years and now features a unique bumpy mixture of asphalt on the straightaways and concrete on the turns. It is the shortest track on the Sprint Cup circuit and it is mostly flat, with only 12-degree banking in the turns.

Managing brakes is very important on this tight course, as crashes are apt to happen at any time. The racing can be physical but the winners need a strategy to escape the mayhem.

As NASCAR grows, the short track of Martinsville is a reminder of the sport's rough-and-tumble early days.

**Michigan International Speedway**
Brooklyn, Michigan
Distance: 2 miles
Layout: D-shaped oval
Seating capacity: 137,243
2007 Races: June 17, Citizens Bank 400
August 19, 3M Performance 400

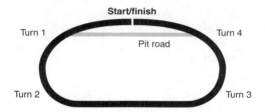

HOT TICKET: Michigan International Speedway is a wide, fairly smooth, two-mile asphalt track that makes for some very exciting side-by-side racing. It has 12-degree banking in the corners and often features long runs with lead changes.

As the home to the automobile manufacturers, this is always a significant race and winning near motor city is important to every driver. After all, the manufacturers are watching and they'd all like to see a win on their home track.

Because of the long runs that this track is known for, fuel strategy is very important.

**New Hampshire International Speedway**
Loudon, New Hampshire
Distance: 1.058 miles
Layout: Oval
Seating Capacity: 91,000
2007 Races: July 1, Lenox Industrial Tools 300
            September 16, Sylvania 300

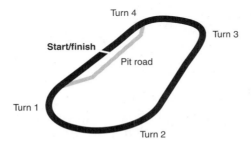

HOT TICKET: New Hampshire International Speedway brings NASCAR to New England on an asphalt course that is referred to as "The Magic Mile." The asphalt course features long straightaways that run into pretty flat 12-degree turns and so braking is a very important skill.

In the tiny, picturesque town of Loudon, the New Hampshire International Speedway has undergone changes to make racing safer. After a couple of fatal accidents in 2000, the apron into one of the turns was widened to create a more sweeping and safer entrance.

New Hampshire features exciting racing but finding a place to pass is difficult.

**Phoenix International Raceway**
Avondale, Arizona
Distance: 1 mile
Layout: Tri-oval
Seating capacity: 76,800
2007 Races: April 21, Subway Fresh Fit 500
 November 11, Checkers Auto Parts 500 Presented
 by Pennzoil

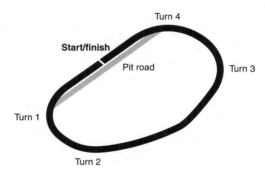

HOT TICKET: Phoenix International Raceway features a dogleg curve on the backstretch that is different than racers see on other tracks. The one-mile asphalt track features variable banking from 9 to 11 degrees.

The corners are mostly flat so brakes come into play but when cars come out of the corners they can fly. The course is a very interesting layout. One other thing that comes into play at Phoenix is the sun aiming into the windshield.

Corners are the places to pay attention at this track because that is where most of the passing occurs.

**Pocono Raceway**
Long Pond Pennsylvania
Distance: 2.5 miles
Layout: Triangular
Seating Capacity: 76,812
2007 Races: June 10, Pocono 500
August 5, Pennsylvania 500

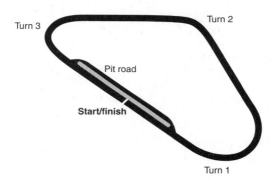

HOT TRACKS: Pocono Raceway is a unique triangular asphalt track with three very different kinds of turns for drivers to negotiate. The corners are banked anywhere from 6 degrees to 14 degrees.

Even the straightaways between the corners vary in length so racing is interesting and different on all parts of the track. Since the course is not an oval or a road course, drivers have taken to calling it a "roval."

Pocono is in a beautiful spot set in the mountains and has even had deer wander across the track.

**Richmond International Raceway**
Richmond, Virginia
Distance: 0.75 mile
Layout: Oval
Seating Capacity: 112,029
2007 Race: May 5, Crown Royal Presents the
Your Name Here (Jim Stewart) 500
September 8, Chevy Rock & Roll 400

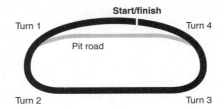

HOT TICKET: Richmond International Raceway, opened in 1951, is the only three-quarter mile track on the Sprint Cup circuit. Races here are unique because it combines some elements of short course racing with some elements of a big track.

The track used to be a half-mile but it was changed in 1988. Races here are interesting because they are night races.

Racing at Richmond is some of the best in the country because of all the unique characteristics, the history, and the atmosphere under the lights.

**Talladega Superspeedway**
Talladega, Alabama
Distance: 2.66 miles
Layout: Tri-oval
Seating capacity: 143,231
2007 Races: April 29, Aaron's 499
             October 7, UAW-Ford 500

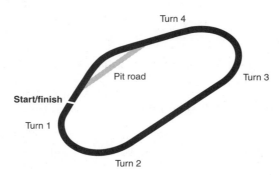

HOT TICKET: Talladega Superspeedway, the largest of NASCAR's tracks, is synonymous with speed. This 2.66-mile asphalt superspeedway with 33-degree banked corners is one of two tracks (Daytona) that requires restrictor plates that limit the horsepower, and thus the speed, of cars.

Strategy in restrictor-plate racing involves drafting, which means teaming up with another driver.

Talladega is so big and restrictor plate racing creates big bunches of cars, so a key strategy is avoiding a big crash by staying out front or behind the group until it's time to move up.

**Texas Motor Speedway**
Fort Worth, Texas
Distance: 1.5 miles
Layout: Oval
Seating Capacity: 159,585
2007 Races: April 15, Samsung 500
               November 4, Dickies 500

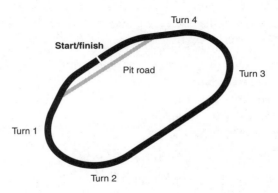

HOT TICKET: Texas Motor Speedway, opened in 1997, is one of the new types of "cookie cutter" racetracks that have a similar look. The 1.5-mile asphalt surface features 24-degree banking in the corners.

Texas is a fast track featuring wide-open racing and therefore, tires and engines are major factors here. Cars can fly into corners at more than 200 miles per hour and then have to slow down as they take the turn.

Located between Dallas and Fort Worth, the Texas Motor Speedway is a huge, fan-friendly facility that offers a fantastic show.

**Watkins Glen International**
Watkins Glen, New York
Distance: 2.45 miles
Layout: 11-turn road course
Seating Capacity: 41,000
2007 Race: August 12, NASCAR Nextel Cup at the Glen

Pit road

Start/finish

HOT TICKET: Watkins Glen International is one of only two road courses (Infineon) on the Sprint Cup circuit. This 11-turn road course challenges drivers to turn right at key points.

With all the turns on this course, drivers must be especially skilled using brakes. The elevation does not change like it does at the other road course, Infineon. Watkins Glen is a flat course that is fast and flowing.

Located in the spectacular Finger Lakes area of upstate New York, this track is an interesting change from most of the circle driving that occurs during the season.

# Safety at the Track

Racing is dangerous. Through the years, tragedy has struck the sport but changes have come to racetracks as NASCAR has responded to tragedy by making improvements. The biggest change in recent years at racetracks has been the introduction of SAFER barrier—the Steel And Foam Energy Reduction system that has been placed over the existing concrete walls. (For more information on safety, see Chapters 2 and 6)

Racing is exciting and the crashes are part of the excitement but racing is also a hero machine and everyone wants to see the heroes race another day.

## The Least You Need to Know

- ◆ There are many different kinds of racetracks.
- ◆ Bristol is brutal.
- ◆ Daytona and Talladega are restrictor plate races.
- ◆ The SAFER barrier has made racing safer.

# Chapter 6

# Inside a Car

## In This Chapter

- ◆ The evolution of the stock racecar
- ◆ The basics of a NASCAR Sprint Cup car
- ◆ Safety features of a car
- ◆ Details of the Car of Tomorrow
- ◆ A word on inspections and cheating

The workplace of a NASCAR driver is different than yours. And although he drives in what is known as a "stock car," there is actually nothing "stock" about his car. His office is a 3,450-pound racing machine.

Sure, racing has always occurred (that's the point!) in NASCAR, but vehicles in the early years were not specialized. "Stock" meant stock. You know, until it didn't.

And now the only "stock" in NASCAR is the nameplate. Everything else is custom-built from the ground up, most likely in some fancy North Carolina garage that serves part-time as a shrine.

And now, NASCAR has taken it a step further. NASCAR spent seven years designing a new custom car called The Car of Tomorrow, which debuted at Bristol Motor Speedway on March 25, 2007.

This new template was planned to be phased-in over two years so that it would be introduced full-time in 2009. But that changed after it was first used and now it will be the full-time car in 2008. It is still being referred to by most people as the Car of Tomorrow although some have tried to make other names stick. Both the old car and the Car of Tomorrow, as you might imagine, are incredible full-fledged racing machines. The differences, though, are significant.

This is a chapter about the car in NASCAR. It will cover the evolution of the car through the years, including the various manufacturers, and then discuss details of the car such as tires, engines, and safety features. This chapter will explain the revolutionary change that is the Car of Tomorrow and finish with a brief look at the inspection process and the history of cheating.

# Evolution of the Car Through the Years

In the beginning, anybody could race. Racers would bring a car, weld their doors shut (or, in some cases, leather belts or rope were used to keep doors closed) and go racing.

Now, racecars don't even have doors. That's just one of the many changes that have occurred through the years.

**Awesome!**

The weight of a Sprint cup car at the beginning of a race is standardized at 3,450 pounds. The weight had been 3,400 pounds, but in June 2007, NASCAR increased the weight by 50 pounds.

So step back in time for a moment to the America of just after World War II and envision the old NASCAR world of strict definition. Stock car. That's what they drove back then. Other than improvised seat belts and door restraints, these cars were the same ones that everyone else in America drove. That was truly crazy, white-knuckle racing.

In 1952, NASCAR mandated roll bars as one of the first safety features used specifically for racing. (The roll bars were replaced by a sturdier roll cage in early 1960s.) Plus, in 1952, two-way radios were introduced. But, although they were not used regularly until much later, the evolution had begun.

But for a long time, NASCAR stayed close to its stock car roots and only small changes for safety's sake were allowed.

Then the manufacturers got involved. And in the early years, there were a lot of manufacturers. In fact, nine different manufacturers entered the first NASCAR race: Buick, Cadillac, Chrysler, Ford, Hudson, Kaiser, Lincoln, Mercury, and Oldsmobile. And each one of them began to notice how racing affected sales.

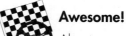

**Awesome!**

About a week before the 1960 Daytona 500, Ray Fox bought a brand new Chevrolet from a showroom floor, made a few changes, and then Junior Johnson drove the car to victory.

In 1953, Hudson drivers won 22 of 37 races after Hudson introduced the twin H carburetor setup. And in 1955, Chevrolet introduced the small block V8 engine. Engine work and suspensions were key in the early years, and especially as the big tracks were being built.

In 1958, Chevrolet introduced the X-frame with coil spring rear suspension that gave the flexibility needed for the new 2.5-mile Daytona International Speedway, which was finished a year later.

In the 1960s as more speedways were built and dirt tracks began to be eliminated, manufacturers began the decade by focusing on engines. But by the end of the decade, all the rage was aerodynamics (see Chapter 2).

In 1981, NASCAR shortened the *wheelbase* from 115 inches to 110 inches. This reflected the shorter styles that were coming into popularity.

**Pit Stop!**

**Wheelbase** is the distance between the center of the front wheel and the center of the rear wheel.

And that shortening of the wheelbase was the last major

design change mandated to a NASCAR cup car until the Car of Tomorrow was introduced on March 25, 2007, at Bristol.

Sure, many other changes occurred through the years. But none were quite as radical as shortening the wheelbase and certainly nothing was as revolutionary as the complete redesign that is the Car of Tomorrow (more later).

But before we examine the Car of Tomorrow and the changes it brings, here is a look at some of the basics of a Sprint Cup car from the ground up.

# Four Manufacturers—Chevrolet, Dodge, Ford, and Toyota

For many years until 2007, there were three manufactures in Sprint Cup racing—Chevrolet, Dodge and Ford. All were American. But in 2007, Japanese automaker Toyota entered.

Chevrolet ran a Monte Carlo in races with the old car, but runs an Impala with the Car of Tomorrow (COT) (see later in this chapter).

Dodge ran a Charger but runs an Avenger with the COT.

Ford runs a Fusion. Toyota runs a Camry.

Manufacturers invest millions of dollars in NASCAR racing. Why? The old cliché is the reason: win on Sunday, sell on Monday. Quite simply, winning helps sell cars (see Chapter 10).

# Race Tires by Goodyear

These tires have no tread. Treadless tires, in fact, grip the dry road better than a tire with a tread. But that's just the beginning of the difference between race tires and your tires.

Race tires (all made by Goodyear) are not filled with air. They are filled with nitrogen because nitrogen does not produce moisture. Moisture is not good because it expands when it gets hotter, which is not a great thing for a car going almost 200 miles per hour.

*(Courtesy of Bryan Hallman.)*

*Race tires.*

Since cars are always turning left, the strain on the right side tires is greater than that on the left side tires. Thus, the right side tire is harder. And, since racetracks are very different, NASCAR teams use different tires at the different racetracks.

Some tracks are concrete, but most are asphalt. Some are bumpy and some are smooth. Some are high banked and others are flat. Some are long superspeedways and other are short ovals, while others are road courses that include right turns. All of this is taken into consideration when choosing tires.

And crews must consider when to take the time to change tires because it is a fine balance. New tires make a car faster. But it takes crucial time to change tires. (More on pit strategy in Chapters 7 and 9.)

# The Engine—a 358 Regulated Monster of Power

All Sprint cup cars have a single engine size—358 cubic inch maximum displacement. It didn't used to be that way. NASCAR once had a complicated formula for engine size that was determined by, among other things, the weight of the vehicle and the aerodynamics of the car.

Current cup cars use cast-iron V8 engines with aluminum cylinder heads. The engines use a special type of racing oil and are designed to withstand extreme heat and long runs.

*(Courtesy of Bryan Hallman.)*

*Look what's under the hood.*

Unlike modern cars, which now use fuel injection, NASCAR mandates the use of a carburetor because they are easier to inspect. Here are a few other Sprint Cup car engine facts:

- ◆ Four-speed transmission

- ◆ Approximately 850 horsepower at 9000 rpm

- ◆ Compression ratio 12:1

- ◆ Sunoco 112 octane fuel

A NASCAR engine is a precision-engineered, tightly regulated monster of power that can make or break a racecar's chances.

These big engines can produce more than 800 horsepower. On small tracks, it would be impossible to use all this power but if one of these engines were let loose on Daytona or especially Talladega, cars could possibly top 230 miles per hour (see Chapter 2).

In an accident, a car could become airborne, making it dangerous for fans. So starting in 1988, NASCAR has mandated that cars use a restrictor plate at those two racetracks.

# Restrictor Plates

Restrictor plates are thin aluminum squares with four holes drilled in them. They are placed between the carburetor and the engine and they restrict the flow of air, which in turn significantly reduces the horsepower to 450.

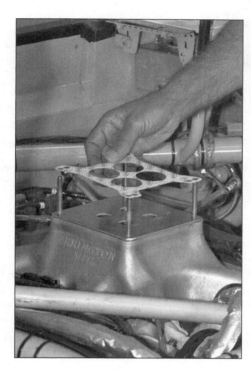

*A restrictor plate is used to reduce horsepower on the superspeedways of Daytona and Talladega.*

*(Courtesy of Bryan Hallman.)*

A reduction in horsepower reduces the speed, which is supposed to then reduce the danger of cars becoming airborne. It is used at only two racetracks—the 2.5-mile Daytona and the 2.66-mile Talladega. The plate keeps speeds just under 200 miles per hour at these tracks.

But the addition of the restrictor plate has had another effect as well as stopping cars from flying through the air. It changed racing at the two racetracks it is used in. Since all cars are restricted equally, racing tends to bunch up and strategy involves teaming up and using drafting (see Chapter 7).

In fact, some argue that the restrictor plate makes racing more dangerous because the cars are so bunched up that when one gets wobbly it
can cause a massive pileup. On the other hand, as long as no one gets
hurt, massive pileups are exciting. In either case, restrictor plate racing
appears to be here to stay.

# Speed Needs Safety

Those aren't Hollywood special effects that you see when the crashes
happen. Those are real—real spectacular and real dangerous.

And so through the years NASCAR has made changes to the car for
safety's sake. Some of those changes have come about only after a
tragedy. Other changes were more proactive. Nevertheless, though
involved in a most dangerous sport, these cars are incredibly safe.

To describe all the safety features on a NASCAR vehicle could probably
take a book itself, and maybe an engineering and chemistry degree. But
here are a few highlights.

## Fuel Cells

Gasoline vapors easily catch on fire so NASCAR has mandated that
all gas tanks be safe-as-possible compartments that contain the vapors
using special foam that stops the liquid from sloshing around. These
special NASCAR gas tanks are called fuel cells.

The tank itself is double lined. The outside is steel and the inside is
a hard rubber. The tanks are difficult to puncture and the foam is
designed to capture the amount of air in the tank so that there is not a
lot of air to help the fuel catch fire. The foam is to keep the fuel from
splashing around in the event of a rupture of the rubber bladder.

In addition, fuels cells are designed to close off immediately in a cata-
strophic accident that turns the car upside down.

## Five-Point Harness

NASCAR drivers always wear their seatbelts. The seatbelts of
NASCAR drivers are much more than waist and shoulder restraints.

They wear five-point restraints of thick padded nylon webbing. Two belts go over the driver's shoulders and meld into one belt between his legs. And a belt goes across his waist, connecting on both sides.

The belts fit very snug as the driver sits in a contoured seat that is designed to also hug his body and protect it during a crash.

## Window Nets

In order to protect drivers during crashes in which they roll, protective netting is on each side-window area of the car. The cars do not have side windows. They have nets.

When a car rolls over, sometimes the forces are so strong that the driver cannot control where his arms go. The net is a strong mesh that keeps drivers' arms inside the car in the event of a crash or rollover.

## Roof Flaps

Two flaps on the roof are designed to go up if the car suddenly spins backward, causing the air pressure on the top of the car to dramatically decrease.

NASCAR learned that this was a situation that caused cars to go airborne so these flaps were installed to automatically react to the situation.

## Head And Neck Support—HANS Device

This device is a collar that is harnessed to the upper body. The collar is then attached to the helmet with two flexible tethers that allow the head some flexibility to drive but prevent it from snapping forward during a wreck.

The HANS device has been mandated since 2001. Four deaths from head injuries, including that of Dale Earnhardt, in the previous year led to the mandate.

# Here Today Is the Car of Tomorrow

In 2007, after seven years of development, evolution became revolution when NASCAR introduced a complete redesign of the car template used in Sprint Cup racing.

The plan was to introduce the car for 16 races in 2007, 26 of the 36 races in 2008 and then all the races in 2009. But NASCAR changed course midway through 2007 and the COT is being introduced full-time for the 2008 season.

With safety as the primary consideration, the Car of Tomorrow (COT) brings revolutionary changes to the chassis of the car as well as to the interior. It also is supposed to help contain costs and improve competition with a design that makes passing easier.

It is, in fact, a radical change that brings a boxy design with some interesting front-and rear-end features.

*(Courtesy of Bryan Hallman.)*

*The Car of Tomorrow in the first race at Bristol, March 25, 2007. Note the boxy design, front splitter, and rear wing.*

The Car of Tomorrow was an unknown going into the 2007 season but as racing began in Bristol and continued part-time through the rest of the season, more became known about how the car would handle and react to various situations.

Most of all, the car is different. Start with the name. The car has been developed for seven years and now it is racing. On one day, March 24, 2007, the name was accurate. There is talk as of press time to changing the name. Ideas floated to rename the car include the Specification Car, the XL car, the New Car, and probably a bunch of others.

# COT Safety Improvements

NASCAR was proactive by designing the Car of Tomorrow.

Many safety changes in NASCAR through the years came after a tragedy and a NASCAR ruling but this new redesign is a researched built-from-the-ground-up racing machine that theoretically took everything into consideration.

This is the first actual NASCAR-designed vehicle. All previous racing vehicles were designed by manufactures and builders to NASCAR's evolving specifications. For the COT, they started from scratch. Here are some highlights.

◆ The driver's seat was moved closer to the center of the car. This moves the driver further away from side impact hits.

◆ There is a double-frame rail with steel plates covering the door bars to prevent intrusion into the cockpit.

◆ The cockpit is bigger and there is $2^1/_2$ inches more headroom.

◆ Energy-absorbing material is installed between the roll cage and the door panels.

# COT Racing Improvements

The Car of Tomorrow is designed to help level the playing field by making one design mandatory for all cars. With the previous car, some teams could afford to design a different car for every racetrack. But this new standard is designed to reduce the ever-skyrocketing costs of racing. There is now a 220 point chassis inspection system that should keep car setups similar.

**Awesome!**

Kyle Busch won the very first race that used the COT. He was not so impressed with his car. He said, "I wanted to go out and win this race so I could tell everybody how terrible this thing is to drive. I can't stand to drive them. They suck."

Some have complained about the boxy design of the COT but it is supposed to cut a hole though the air and to lessen the impact of aerodynamic wind currents from multiple cars traveling at NASCAR speed on the track. It has been compared to the truck and it is four inches wider and two inches taller than the old car design.

Besides the boxy design, two features in particular make the COT very different than the old car.

## The Front Splitter Tunes the Front Down Forces

On the bottom front of the car is a splitter that catches air closest to the track and pushes the front end down, keeping the car on the track. It looks like a shelf.

This splitter is adjustable and can reduce or add the amount of air being caught. The two factors taken into consideration for this adjustment are driver preference and the particular racetrack. Adjusting the splitter will adjust how the racecar drives.

The real adjustment, though, will be the tuning of the splitter with the rear wing, which will give the car the balance a driver desires.

## The Rear Wing Tunes the Rear Down Forces

At the back of the COT, bolted to the top rear is a wing that now takes the place of the old spoiler. This sticks up and out from the car and can also be adjusted to driver preference and racetrack.

One feature of the wing is that it reduces the turbulent air trailing behind the COT. This makes cleaner air behind the car, and thus it should make passing easier.

# COT Marketing

Auto manufacturers are getting a much bigger bulletin board display of their brand on the COT than on the old car. And these cars will more closely resemble the street versions than the old cars.

Plus, the side of the wing is already for rent as a billboard for corporate logos. The wing itself may be next.

# Split-Personality Driving

Two completely different designs were used in 2007 and that was a headache for some drivers. Just getting used to a brand new car, one of the most radical changes in NASCAR history, was difficult enough. Many drivers complained, some famously complained.

The car was introduced anyway. In the 2007 season, drivers were forced to drive two different kinds of cars and that created an even bigger strain on the teams preparing the cars. Teams had to prepare for every race and still try to continue to learn the COT. Because of these concerns, NASCAR adjusted and will run only the COT for the 2008 season.. So check the calendar. Tomorrow is here.

# A Word About Car Inspections

There are lots of rules in NASCAR. Name a car part, including the fuel, and there's a rule. There is some flexibility in the rules sometimes and there is certainly evolution in the rules. Not only that but drivers are always trying to take advantage of anything that is left open to interpretation.

The 2007 NASCAR Nextel Cup rulebook is 184 pages long, and every year it seems to get longer. (In 2005, it was 96 pages.) And since there are rules, there are officials who enforce the rules. The only way to do that is to inspect the car.

Each race is staffed by about 50 officials, who first inspect cars before the race, and then keep an eye on things in pit row.

The car undergoes a vigorous inspection for both safety and fairness. (And the inspection has changed with the Car of Tomorrow.) The standings, in terms of points, determine which car gets inspected first. So cars wait in line to go through the tent and get inspected at various stations.

# Cheating and Punishment

The oldest cliché in NASCAR always read, "If you ain't cheating, you ain't trying."

Much like the bootlegging of lore (see Chapter 2), cheating has always been part of a wink-wink subculture that loves its outlaws and applauds those who are able to sneak their way past that pesky rulebook.

But as NASCAR has grown into a major sport attracting millions of viewers (and dollars), the rulebook has become more and more sacred. If the sport is to maintain its credibility, the rules must be enforced.

In recent years, NASCAR has increased penalties for cheating. And while upholding the rules makes sense for every reason, there is still a part of NASCAR that loves its cheaters.

**Awesome!**

Before the 2007 Daytona 500, cheating was big news. Suspensions and fines were levied against crew members for Kasey Kahne, Elliot Sadler, Scott Riggs, and Matt Kenseth. Michael Waltrip was fined an unprecedented $100,000 and docked 100 driver points for adding something illegal to his fuel. Waltrip's vice president and crew chief were suspended indefinitely.

In fact, one of the most notorious and most fined cheaters of all time, Robin Pemberton, is now the NASCAR Vice President of Competition. Pemberton, who currently helps set and enforce the rules, was once fined $40,000 for putting a carburetor spacer plate in Mark Martin's car at Richmond. Pemberton is not the first former cheater to enforce the rules. He replaced Gary Nelson, who was a well-known rule bender of his era.

And so it goes in NASCAR, or at least so it went. The stories of illegal manifolds and radical chassis design and extra fuel and fuel additives, and even a device that actually dropped lead buckshot so a car became lighter during a race, are some of the cheating stories of yesteryear that have led NASCAR to where it is now.

It's, in fact, easy to make a case that cheating has made NASCAR better by the simple fact that cheating created much of the rule book.

One particular early mechanic and car designer, Henry "Smokey" Yunick, estimated that in 1970 half the NASCAR rulebook was dedicated to him. Yunick, like everyone in NASCAR, was looking to take advantage of gray areas and he was one of the best ever.

But it seems to never end. In the 2007 season, three of the most famous driver's teams were caught cheating on the COT.

◆ At Darlington Raceway, Dale Earnhardt Jr.'s car had illegal brackets on the rear wing and he was docked 100 points. His crew chief, Tony Eury Jr., was suspended for six races and fined $100,000.

◆ At Infinion Raceway, Jeff Gordon and Jimmie Johnson had illegal modifications to the front fenders on each of their cars. Each was docked 100 points. Gordon's crew chief Steve Letarte and Johnson's crew chief Chad Knauss were suspended for six races and fined $100,000.

## The Least You Need to Know

◆ Sprint Cup cars are precision-built racing machines, not stock cars.

◆ Tires, made by Goodyear, do not have tread.

◆ The engine is a 358 cubic inch V8.

◆ Cars are very safe and continually developing.

◆ The Car of Tomorrow is a radical new design with safety in mind.

◆ Cheating, long part of NASCAR lore, is now severely punished.

# Chapter 7

# Race Strategy

## In This Chapter

- ◆ Why strategy is important, the competition is close
- ◆ Pre-race strategy
- ◆ In-race adjustments
- ◆ The role of communication
- ◆ The importance of pit stops

How is a race won? The answer is always the same—just finish first.

Other than that, race strategy is a conundrum wrapped around a riddle going almost 200 miles an hour. How is a race won? Let us count the ways … er, what number comes after infinity?

There are an infinite number of ways to win a race because the variables involved are almost infinite. Plus, every racetrack is different. And they act different on different days.

Those living variables—such as the weather, and what other drivers do, and when or if there is a crash or a caution or a million other situations—all figure into the complicated hoped-for equation that always includes luck and creates an opportunity-to-thank-the-sponsor victory. How do you win a race? By saying, *"I couldn't have done it without my sponsor."*

But how is a race really won? By finishing first. After that, the only real answer is to be smart, good, and lucky. And having money and a lot of cars and teammates helps a lot. Race strategy is a chief reason why racing is so popular—there's just so much to it.

This chapter will cover the basics of race strategy, including pre-race preparations and in-race adjustments, touching on the role of communication and the supreme importance of pit stop decisions. It will cover some track-specific considerations including superspeedway drafting. And this chapter will touch on the racing that occurs at the end of a race, and the ongoing temptation to cheat.

# An Evenly Matched Field Requires Strategy

The top qualifier in a Sprint Cup race usually beats the 44th car (only 43 qualify—see Chapter 4) by less than half a second on a one-car-only timed lap of the track. The competition is that brutally close and therefore every edge—any edge—is supremely important.

It is a long 10-month season and sometimes 60 cars are trying to qualify for those 43 spots—and 35, maybe 36—are already guaranteed (see Chapter 4).

So the car owner, corporations sponsoring the car, and the driver and crew are essentially betting millions of dollars that a particular car can get into a race and then succeed. They wouldn't make the bet if they didn't think that they had a chance. That's how close the field is. Tenths, sometimes hundredths of a second separate the top qualifier from just missing the race entirely.

But that's just the qualifying. Once the race begins, new differences emerge. These differences come from the infinite strategic possibilities, how teams operate, and what decisions are made when—and by whom.

The driver plays a huge role in whether a race is won. But he is only part of the story.

# Pre-Race Strategy

A lot of important strategy happens before the race starts. Although strategy is organic and many changes and decisions are made throughout the race, there is also an enormous amount of pre-race planning that occurs.

Sprint Cup racing is very different than the Strictly Stock car days (see Chapter 2) of early NASCAR when one man would show up with a car and go racing. Now, everything that can possibly be planned is planned. Everything.

One reason for this is that there is so much that cannot be planned for. Another reason is that racing is so close and the cars, drivers, teams, and technology are so similar that any little advantage might just be enough to win a race.

But perhaps the biggest reason why everything is planned is because racing guys are smart enough to have figured out every intricate detail that can help them even by a millionth of a second. If you add enough millionths together, goes the thinking, you may have enough to win a race.

So before a car goes anywhere near a race, everything on the car is tested—wind tunnel tested, laboratory tested, and test-track tested. Calculations are made. Past races and past performances are studied and everyone on the team works to improve the car and themselves. In some ways, the team and the car are one, looking for something that works best. Yet, sometimes, the track simply dictates *setup*.

In modern NASCAR, owners often own more than one car, and therefore, information is shared about how cars perform on a particular racetrack. This can be helpful to multi-car owners who can test different setups and then share information.

**Pit Stop!**

The **setup** of a car is a description of how the many variables—such as shocks, springs, and chassis adjustments—are set before and during a race.

## Racetrack Considerations

Every racetrack is different and each racetrack's characteristics are well known by all. Although some tracks share characteristics, each track is unique and there is a lot to consider when preparing a car including:

- Track distance
- Track layout
- Track surface
- Track banking
- Track width
- Pit area configuration
- Does it require a restrictor plate?
- Average number of cautions

**Awesome!**

One of the biggest pre-race considerations—choosing tires—is now taken care of by Goodyear. Goodyear makes track-specific tires for Sprint Cup racing and tires are different on the left side than on the right because of the constant left turns.

All of these things are important for the team to consider as the car is going through its initial setup. The way the car runs into and out of turns is key, so springs and shocks and tire pressure are among the many factors that are considered to get the car ready to start in what is hoped to be premium shape.

Of course, in racing you never know. And there is so much more to consider than just the particular racetrack or even the particular racetrack on a specific day.

Once qualifying is finished, the starting positions are assigned from the fastest car to the slowest car. Teams get to choose their pit based on their starting position—with the driver of the fastest car choosing first. Pit selection also figures into the team strategy.

## Driver's Racing Style

Every driver is different. Some are aggressive and only feel comfortable if they are up front. Others can bide their time and wait for the long race to develop before they make their move so that car may be planned to trail traffic early on.

Many styles are used, and since five points are awarded for leading a lap, as well as five more for leading the most laps, drivers also take that into consideration. Of course, the most important consideration is the big points (and check) waiting at the end.

**Awesome!**

Driver Matt Kenseth has a strategy of trying to gain an extra five points every race by staying on the racetrack when everyone else pits. This allows him to lead at least one lap during the race, earning five points. Over the season (see Chapter 4), those points add up.

But one pre-race consideration even beyond the specific driving style in the race is the way the driver prefers the car to handle. Again, all drivers are different and a car that is right for one particular driver may be set up all wrong for another. One driver may like a car a bit looser while another may want it tighter.

Plus drivers and crew understand that as the race starts, everything changes. For instance, as the race goes on, tires wear out until they are replaced. And worn tires act differently than new tires. New tires are faster than old tires. They have better grip.

Strategy changes as the handling of the car changes and each driver's ability to handle the ever-changing car is constantly tested.

# In-Race Adjustments, Big Picture

The race is live, and that actually means that it is living and changing. Things happen as the race develops and as the racecar warms up and the tires heat up and begin to wear. Often the best condition the car is in all day is at the beginning of the race. NASCAR racing is tough on cars.

But although the car may be in the best condition of the day, there is no guarantee it will start out in the exact proper setup for an optimum run. Even with all the preparation work, it may take race time to get everything set exactly right.

So unless there is a crash at the beginning of the race (not so unusual), the first thing a driver and crew are doing is simply evaluating. They are evaluating everything because they want to know what they have—and they want to know as much as they can know about what they have on this particular racetrack.

Part of the idea is so that, when it is time to go in and get gas and/or tires, they can also make adjustments to how the car is running.

But also, the crew chief and driver can maybe figure out a way to drive a car a little different while the race is in progress. What does that mean? Here's a simple example—changing how hard he brakes going into corners, or maybe taking a slightly different angle or even—on certain racetracks—a different *racing groove*.

All of it is open for interpretation by the driver and the crew chief. The dynamics of every team are different and yet each team is somehow able to decide together what is to be done to the car and when.

Who ultimately decides? Usually the crew chief decides but it depends on the driver and the situation.

## Communication, Big Picture

The driver and the crew chief talk. For the entire race, they talk on a two-way radio. Although the driver is not ordering pizza, you could say he is placing an order. And you could also say the crew chief is interpreting the order, not following orders. It's a complicated relationship.

Communication has become an essential part of NASCAR racing. The relationship between the driver and the crew chief can take years to develop to the point where the driver can describe the car so that the crew chief can find the exact right changes.

*(Courtesy of Jeff Robinson.)*

*Communication between a driver and crew chief is a key to winning.*

All drivers have come up through the ranks from small tracks where radio communication is nonexistent. They have each proven themselves as a driver. But the top levels of racing are different and communication is an essential part of an entire race because little (or big) adjustments can make the difference between winning and losing.

So they talk. And actually, the driver does most of the talking. Although there are moments in the race when the driver may wander off topic, for the most part the conversation is about the racecar. What is it doing? When is it doing it? Drivers (see Chapter 8) have an extraordinary feel for what a car can do and what it cannot do in what circumstances all over the track.

Meanwhile, no one knows the car better than the crew chief. And he is getting feedback about the car not only from the driver, but also from the team's *spotter.*

### Pit Stop!

The **spotter** is placed high above the racetrack with a radio and serves as a second set of eyes for the driver. The spotter can see the whole track with something of a helicopter view and alert the driver to many situations including crashes, faster drivers approaching, or other drivers dueling in front of him.

The spotter keeps the driver alert as to his helicopter view of the entire racetrack and especially any safety issues. He also reacts to what the driver is saying in describing his car and confirms what the driver is describing about the performance of the car. The spotter, who most likely has been a driver himself, is just a second set of eyes and he speaks when necessary.

*(Courtesy of Bryan Hallman.)*

*A spotter has a helicopter view of the whole race and he tells the driver what he sees.*

But most of the conversation is between the crew chief and the driver. If they work together in perfect synch, they can get the best out of the car—but only if they work together in perfect synch.

It has been said that it can take years for a crew chief and driver to communicate at a championship level and it has also been said that the relationship between the driver and the crew chief is like that of a marriage—two people working toward one grand goal. But how do they do it? What do they talk about? And why is it like a marriage?

Well, if a particular driver and crew chief can, together, figure out how to make their car handle a little bit better and go a little bit faster, they have an advantage. That's what they talk about. But the driver is trying to explain what he feels and what he wants and the crew chief is trying to interpret his words and even his tone of voice so he knows what needs to be done.

But it's even more than that. They don't just talk about what to do. They also talk about when to do it.

## Pit Strategy, Big Picture

A car can never run an entire race without stopping. It needs gas and tires along the way—more than once, in fact—and when it stops for gas and tires, other adjustments can be made to help the handling and performance of the car. That's where the communication comes in. What adjustments? And when?

Earlier in this chapter, you learned about some pre-race considerations. Well, these are also part of the developing strategy because, for instance, the small racetracks—especially Bristol and Martinsville—are known for having a lot of cautions. And all teams know this ahead of time.

Another racetrack, Darlington, has a very coarse surface and so new tires will be needed often. All teams know this ahead of time.

Some of the "cookie cutter" racetracks (see Chapter 5) that were built recently and have a similar design can become three or even four lanes wide in some spots. And all teams know this ahead of time as well.

There is a lot of knowledge that all teams possess ahead of time. But what each team plans to do with that knowledge may be a different story entirely. There are, again, an infinite number of considerations, including driver preferences and the ever-changing situations that come into play in deciding when to pit and what to do when you get there. That's strategy— when to pit and what to do when you get there. The team has only a few seconds for some gas, and two tires or maybe four—or maybe none. When do you do it? How much do you need or want?

# In-Race Adjustments, Some Details

Before the race, a team starts by studying that particular track at that time of year. How many pit stops are needed? How many average cautions are there? What specifically, if anything, is there to expect?

From there forward, everything is geared toward the last pit stop and trying to outsmart the other teams. And in that part of the equation, four key interrelated things come into play.

- ◆ New tires are the fastest tires, but changing tires takes time in the pit.

- ◆ Track position is crucial because passing is so difficult.

- ◆ Coming out of the pit first leads to better track position.

- ◆ Not going into the pit leads to the best track position.

So the question: two tires, four tires, or no tires?

Gas? Other adjustments? Maybe the car got banged up on the track and needs some quick body work or something needs to actually be fixed. Whatever the reason, the car will need to pit in the race and that, often, is where race strategy is especially important. But why?

## A Word About the Rules of Pit Row

Here's what to consider about pit row.

- ◆ There are slotted positions, lined up one by one, along pit row. Some slots are better than others. Drivers with the fastest qualifying times get to choose their pit location first.

- ◆ Cars must park in their slot. If they miss, they can be penalized a lap.

- ◆ There is a speed limit leading out of pit row. The speed limit is different at different tracks because some pit rows, like some tracks, are short. And some are long. Pit row speed limits reflect that. A shorter pit row has a slower speed limit.

- ◆ If cars pit during a caution, they line up behind the pace car in the order that they exit pit row. Thus, getting out of pit row faster than another car improves track position for when the green flag flies and the racing begins again.

## Communication, Some Details

They talk about how the car is handling. Why?

Races are won and lost in the turns because that is where passing is set up. How a car goes into a turn, goes through the turn, and comes out of it is the most important part of the handling of the car. And each aspect of a corner is different as the weight of the car pushes to the outside around the turn. Balance becomes key to handling.

But there is even more to consider than that because, remember, each racetrack is different. Some are banked higher, some flatter. Some turns are tight, some are sweeping. And a couple of tracks in the Sprint Cup circuit—Infineon and Watkins Glen—are road courses that include right turns. All of this makes a difference.

But a generic left turn at NASCAR speeds is still something worth talking about. And two particular terms come up a lot when discussing the handling in the corner—*loose* and *tight*.

**Pit Stop!**

A car is **loose** in a turn when, as it goes around the turn, the back end wants to slide out of control. The phenomenon of *loose* is much like a car going down a snowy street, turning the wheel sideways and sliding sideways down the street.

A car is **tight** when it goes into the turn and the car tends to want to go straight instead of flow into the turn.

Ideally, a driver wants the car to handle somewhere between loose and tight so that it flows through the turn and the driver has perfect control. But what is perfect control in a NASCAR race?

Perfect control is that place at the edge of disaster that most of us wouldn't dare go near because we would obliterate that line and then, most likely, the car. But a NASCAR driver has a special relationship with his car and he can feel how it holds the road in what has been called a traction circle. Hold the traction, but not too much. That's the goal of a good turn.

It's a difficult-to-decipher tipping point but a good driver knows it and he also knows when the car is not performing as it should. And so he describes things like "loose" and "tight" about how his car handles in the corners.

The crew is trying to give a car optimum performance all through the turn and the driver is trying to describe exactly what is happening to the car as it goes through the turn so that adjustments can be made.

**Pit Stop!**

The **track bar** connects the rear end to the chassis and prevents the chassis from swaying side to side. The height of this attachment has a lot to do with whether the car is loose or tight. Lowering the track bar will make the car tighter, and raising it will make it looser.

Well, here's one thing they talk about, the *track bar.* Some drivers know what they want done to the track bar, some think they know, and others might just launch into a general complaint about cornering.

Plus remember that it might handle fine going into a turn but not so well going out. But making a change to how it performs on the way out of the turn could affect how it performs on the way into the turn. Or vice versa. Any adjustment, after all, affects the car for the entire time it is on the track.

And all drivers have somewhat different preferences on how they like their car to handle. So they talk to the crew chief, describing the car and how it is handling. Some drivers (see Chapter 8) are better at describing the car than others.

But the true key to the communication is the relationship between the driver and crew chief. The crew chief has to understand what the driver is saying. He must also understand what it might mean if the driver isn't saying something. Again, like a marriage. The crew chief is interpreting his driver's voice and his mood and what is working and what isn't working (more in Chapter 8).

Together, they make a decision as to what to do and when to do it. They are a team and they must trust each other but when a final decision must be made, the crew chief makes it—unless the driver overrules him. Remember, the driver still has to pull in the pits, or not.

# Pit Strategy, Some Details

A key question of strategy is when to pit and what to do when you get there. Since racetrack knowledge (including the number of average cautions) is common knowledge, each team is playing a game of chess against the other.

As the race develops, certain cars are clearly faster than others. Crashes do happen. Pre-race strategy was nice but when the racing starts, it's time to think on the fly.

And yet pre-race strategy still comes into play during the race because things are geared toward that final pit stop and getting in best position with the fastest tires and at least enough gas to finish. So planning helps, but planning is based on probabilities and guessing what your opponents might do. Much of it aimed at taking a final pit stop at the right time and then making the best and quickest use of it.

But what happens at the final pit stop depends on what has happened at previous pit stops. And teams often choose to pit when there is a caution. But not always. This means that approaching a final pit stop, many teams are in similar condition as far as needing tires or gas.

There are many variations on a strategy of being in position to win.

◆ Pitting earlier than others for tires in order to stay on the track for track position when others pit. The danger in this is that those with newer tires will be faster.

◆ Pitting and only getting two tires. Two new tires can help some and changing only two tires helps the car out of pit row faster and into a better track position. The danger is four new tires are faster than two new tires. And drivers getting no tires have better track position.

◆ Pitting and getting four tires. Four new tires are faster, but take the longest, meaning track position will most likely be lost.

◆ Not pitting during green and only waiting for a caution to pit. Staying on the track is good, although older tires go slower. Plus, there are no guaranteed cautions, only guesswork.

◆ Not pitting during a caution and staying in good track position. This gains track position versus gaining speed from new tires or adjustments.

There are other variations on all of this and other considerations as well, such as an impending storm that may cancel the race and cause the leader to be declared the winner. In this case, strategy involves weather forecasting.

The list of considerations is almost endless as the race develops. And a crew chief must make these calls. He bases his call on everything he sees, everything he has learned through experience, everything he is hearing from his driver, and also simply on his instincts.

He must be smart and wise and yet gutsy and courageous. As crew chiefs gain experience they can lose some of their willingness to take a chance and so, often, they will keep younger crewmembers around just to keep fresh ideas always in their head. Wisdom alone is not enough. There must be the energy of innovation and discovery as well. How does a crew chief know if the call he made was the right one? Only when he is in *Victory Lane*.

> **Pit Stop!**
>
> **Victory Lane** is where the winning racecar is taken after a race to celebrate and get presented with some kind of reward.

But the path to Victory Lane is not an easy one. It is filled with pitfalls and potential problems. One of the biggest problems is the very real possibility that the car won't be around at the end of the race.

# Survival

There is attrition during a Sprint Cup race. Every race is different but all racers know this essential rule of strategy: you can't win if your car won't run.

So mixed in with everything else that the driver and crew must think about is how to survive. Of course, the first way to survive is to hang back and wait out the crashes and then pick a spot and time to begin to try to move up. That's a dangerous strategy because hanging back could begin to mean far back, even a lap back.

A second strategy is to just get in the middle of it and trust your luck and instincts. That is dangerous by its nature and yet at some point in the race it is absolutely necessary.

*Staying out of crashes is good strategy.*

The best strategy by far is to take the lead and stay there the entire race—in front of any possible fracas. The problem is that everyone else knows this strategy too. This makes most drivers, while pursuing this strategy, rely on the second strategy (see previous paragraph).

There are two aspects of this that are incredibly important—luck and skill. Luck involves not getting in an inescapable situation. And skill means that the driver is adept at seeing and steering around any accidents he can escape from. Some of the near misses are dramatic and, again, display the incredible skill of the drivers (more in Chapter 8).

But survival is about more than surviving accidents. It's about having the car—the engine specifically—survive. Engines can and do burn out.

## Everything Changes Near the End of a Race

There comes a time during the quest to survive a race that a racer realizes he has a legitimate shot to win. Now, of course, that situation may exist throughout the entire race but there is still something different that happens during the final laps.

The final 20 laps? The final 10? The final 5? The final lap? It's an indecipherable time, although it may be from the final pit stop on, but something happens at the end of a race that ramps up the action, the racing, and the drama. What happens? It's easy to figure out. Everyone with a chance to win decides it's time to take that chance. And what was progression around the track suddenly becomes a battle.

When to make the move is important because, much like in boxing, there is often a counter punch coming and some say being in front in certain races is like being a sitting duck, waiting to be passed. This is especially true in restrictor plate races where drafting takes place and cars can team up in what race announcer and NASCAR driving legend Darrell Waltrip calls "co-opitition"—a mix of cooperation and competition.

*(Courtesy of Bryan Hallman.)*

*Teammates Jeff Gordon and Jimmie Johnson.*

On a superspeedway where cars are limited by the restrictor plate, two cars together can go faster than one car alone. And so, cars team up (often teammates with the same owner, or sometimes cars of the same manufacturer) in order to pass another car. But, again, as the end is in sight, competition trumps cooperation and yet cooperation is still needed. It's a tricky business out on the racetrack, especially near the end.

## Thinking Big Picture for the Cup Chase

Yet one other thing comes into play as well. Cars want to survive and finish in order to get points to qualify for the Chase for the Sprint Cup at the end of the season (see Chapter 4).

So as much as winning counts, finishing and getting points also counts. That's where racing and banging are weighed against the big picture of getting enough points to be one of the 12 racers that qualify for the Chase.

# Another Word About Cheating

Is cheating part of strategy? No. But the famous gray area in the rules is. If it's open for interpretation, then it is certainly open for interpretation—wink, wink, nudge, nudge.

But as NASCAR has grown, cheating is not tolerated and the sport holds vigorous pre- and post-race inspections to catch cheaters. And punishment is getting more severe, including suspensions of crewmembers and even penalizing points.

## The Least You Need to Know

- ◆ The competition is close; strategy is important.
- ◆ The racetrack and its design are strategic considerations.
- ◆ Handling in the turns is the key to car adjustments.
- ◆ When to pit and what to do when you get there is the key strategic decision.

# Chapter 8

# The Superstar in the Car

## In This Chapter

- ◆ An explanation of the many jobs of a driver
- ◆ Typical paths to glory
- ◆ Why Wendell Scott matters
- ◆ An examination of on-track skills
- ◆ An examination of off-track duties

Focus here. A NASCAR driver is the focal point and in that capacity he carries much responsibility—and is paid accordingly. And why is that? Focus.

The car, of course, is—literally—in his hands. And that responsibility of the car as test of absolute focus, hand-eye coordination, and endurance is what makes the driver the focus of the race. All the other stuff—the crew, the track, even the car—somehow lose out to thoughts of that particular human being at that particular moment. We inevitably think of *the driver*.

And in that moment of vicarious transference, all of his other responsibilities—as a businessman/celebrity—come into focus. There's that word again. It seems to float around a driver like one of the many camera lenses examining his life.

This is a chapter about the job of a NASCAR driver and his role both on and off the track. This chapter will first examine multiple roles of a driver and then delve into some of his skills on the track and the typical up-through-the-ranks stories of how drivers begin. It will also cover the salesman, businessman, and celebrity aspects of the modern driver's life.

# Not Multi-Tasking; Super-Tasking

A NASCAR driver doesn't just drive a car for a living. Driving is part of his job—and, in fact, the reason for the other parts of his job—but it's far from the only task that earns his big paycheck. The modern NASCAR driver is actually a human corporation with many departments. He doesn't so much multi-task as he super-tasks—one task at a time with laser focus. And then he moves on.

Part of the corporation, of course, drives the car. Another part works with the crew chief to lead the team. Another part works with the owner on the bigger picture as part of the owner's corporation of a few cars and drivers. And of course, the driver must work with the other teams and drivers. But the driver as a corporation also has a sales department that has to at least cooperate with R&D before going out to meet the customers—er, fans. The corporation that is a NASCAR driver is able, with super focus, to do one thing and then another thing and do them all very well.

Focus. Get it yet? The role of a driver is to have the best-ever focus. After all, the concrete wall is about two inches away on the right, while the red car is about two inches away on the left. Focus? When he is on the racetrack that job is obvious—though maybe not as obvious as you think (more later).

But there is a lot more to his job than when he is on the racetrack. He also has to be very good at pleasing the owner, his crew chief and teammates, his sponsor, and his fans. When he is doing all that other stuff—what is he great at? Very good—it's focus!

# Paths to Glory

Maybe it was a go-kart. Or maybe it was the first time he ever saw a race. More likely, it had to do with family, background, location, and environment—and then it had to do with drive, talent and, oh yeah, focus.

Anyway, out on some local track somewhere this particular driver proved he was good. And then the magical thing happened—somebody noticed and decided to give him a chance to move up.

Every driver has their own particular path to glory but the basics of going up through the ranks remain the same for all of them. Getting an opportunity is the key.

There are lots of good drivers, and a few great drivers—but far fewer opportunities. Perhaps the best driver ever is someone you've never heard of. It's possible. We'll never know because there are so few of these multi-million-dollar cars to drive.

But there are a lot of local tracks and there are many other organizing bodies beyond NASCAR. And while some drivers with great talent may never get the opportunity to get noticed by the right people, they all know that the way up is through the local tracks—in some kind of car or another.

Not all NASCAR drivers began in just stock cars but all began somewhere smaller than the Sprint Cup circuit. And that's where each one first started to win. Of course, there are a lot of small tracks in America and that means there are many winners. But only a few get chosen to move up. Chosen? Chosen by whom?

Car owners (for more, see Chapter 10) are always looking for young talented drivers who can move up through the various series (see Chapter 3).

The mix of drivers in Sprint Cup racing is a blend of experienced and younger drivers. A handful of drivers are household names—superstars known even beyond NASCAR. About half the field is well known to all race fans. And the other half might be new, or they might be what some fans call "recycled drivers"—that is, drivers who have driven at this level before with some, but not a lot, of success.

Some drivers are lucky enough to come from racing families (see Chapter 11). And yet, even if a driver is born with a famous last name, he still has to prove himself on the racetrack. But a young racer from a famous racing family has a built-in advantage—if he's good he will get a chance. Others, just as good, might not be so lucky.

**Awesome!**

New drivers want to impress so they tend to be aggressive and crash more. Experienced drivers know how to stay out of crashes, but sometimes don't take chances necessary to produce victory.

The reasons why one driver gets picked and another does not are as varied as the owners doing the choosing. Choosing a driver is like hiring someone only it is even a bigger thing. It is a bet. The owner is betting that the driver has "it"... whatever it is. And it's not just about winning either— it's about winning *and* charisma.

Drivers are not just drivers. Drivers are celebrities—and salesmen, well, actually pitchmen. And so all of that goes into the equation of how drivers are chosen. But another big part of it is simply opportunity. Location plays a big part. A local driver far away from the NASCAR epicenter in North Carolina may have a harder time getting noticed by the right people.

Driving skills do get noticed. But sometimes a driver simply has to move to get noticed—and to find more competition. The paths to glory are many and they continue to change through the years. Early on, the path to glory was through moonshine (see Chapter 2). But no matter how they got there, one thing is true of all of them—they sure can drive.

# Why Wendell Scott Matters

There are a lot of famous names in NASCAR (see Chapters 2 and 11) but perhaps none carries the weight of Wendell Scott, whose best season was in 1966 when he finished sixth in points. Just sixth?

Scott, who died in 1990, was the first African-American driver in the top level of NASCAR and endured as much or more than baseball's first black player, Jackie Robinson.

Scott was a former taxi driver who was known by local police as a great moonshine driver (see Chapter 2). In 1949, when a promoter was looking for an African-American driver to appear at the Danville Fairgrounds, local police recommended Scott. That was the beginning of his career and by 1961 he managed to get to the top level of NASCAR, which at the time was called the Grand National Series (see Chapter 2).

Scott's legend endures even as NASCAR is trying to grow. It's trying with a lot of money but one unfortunate fact from its past cannot be ignored. Almost all of its drivers from history—since 1947 (see Chapter 2)—have been white men. Wendell Scott is an important exception and a trailblazer.

# Racetrack Qualities

Alert and focused—one with the racecar for four hours in 98-degree heat without a bathroom break or even a timeout. Is a driver an athlete? Well, he sure is something special.

He drives almost 200 miles an hour just inches away from other cars or a concrete wall—or maybe both. He does this for hours. No, this is not a typical Sunday drive. But for a NASCAR driver, that's exactly what it is—a Sunday drive. Of course, no Sunday in NASCAR is typical. All Sundays are special … just like the drivers.

But the key reason he is able to drive on Sunday is because of what he has proven he can do on the track with his combination of driving skill, courage, mental toughness, and endurance.

## Driving Skill

You learned a bit about "loose" and "tight" and controlling the racecar to the edge of losing it in Chapter 7. Drivers have a special feel for all of this and more in their racecar. They can feel the race develop and sense the other drivers as they round the track.

But there is much that they don't know and can't sense, and so they must simply react. The driving skills of the driver are always very much *in the moment*. And yet, it is almost not really conscious driving, but rather subconscious—reacting without thinking.

But the complexity is a bit deeper still because there is a very conscious effort on top of that to execute a specific yet evolving plan (see Chapter 7).

**Pit Stop!**

**Hitting the marks** is what a driver is trying to do around each turn, which is hit a certain spot on the racetrack on the way into the turn and on the way out. This "hitting the marks" assures consistency throughout the turn.

And wrapped in all of this thinking and reacting is the driving itself. There are a lot of parts to it. For one thing, drivers are constantly talking about *hitting the marks*.

But as he is trying to hit his marks he knows that other drivers are also trying to hit marks—maybe the same ones. Plus, everyone knows that the time to take a chance is on the turn by either going high or going low. It's a complicated game of cat and mouse between drivers and it also involves blocking as well as the concept of a premium lap by hitting marks. Each driver is always aiming for a premium lap, and it may be a different way around the track from driver to driver, and even from lap to lap.

Driving skill is the instinctual yet wise ability to figure it all out based on talent and knowledge. It's the difference to understanding the contact sport of a track such as Bristol versus the drafting strategy of Talladega or Daytona.

Driving skill is even more than driving, of course. It's an ability to describe the car (see Chapter 7) in detail so that the crew chief can make appropriate changes. The modern driver is a skilled communicator. The more descriptive the driver is about his car, the more help he offers to the crew chief. So as the driver is fighting his way through each lap, he is also describing the car and looking for big picture advice from the spotter (see Chapter 7).

**Awesome!**

A couple of decades ago, before radios were common, drivers would communicate about the condition of their car by hitting their car with their hand out the window. The crew chief would watch down the straightaway and if the driver hit the door, his car was loose. If he reached and hit the roof, it was tight.

But driving skill actually means a little something different than it did in years past when a driver had to literally manhandle his car through a turn.

Sure, even in a modern car the steering will sometimes become difficult. But the driver usually feels the car on the road rather than overpowering the car with his strength on the wheel. It's a real difference.

The driver is always thinking through his specific situation and trying to understand how the race is developing in accordance with his pre-race strategy (see Chapter 7) on the particular racetrack. There are, in fact, a couple of strategic in-race moves that occur at two different types of racetracks:

- ◆ Superspeedway drafting occurs in restrictor plate (see Chapter 6) racing at Talladega and Daytona. Drivers know that two cars together, because of the aerodynamics, go faster than one car alone. Therefore drivers need partners to team up with and then they have to be cold-hearted enough to break away from the partner when it is time to win. Sometimes, the driver behind will actually bump into the rear bumper of the car in front. This push—called "bump drafting"—propels the car in front forward and it ends up making both cars faster. When done correctly, it is very effective. But it is very dangerous when done wrong.

- ◆ The bump and run occurs usually at small tracks, especially Bristol and Martinsville. This technique involves a trailing car bumping the back bumper of the leading car just enough so that the lead driver has to struggle to regain control. Meanwhile, the trailing driver cruises right past him.

And yet for all of his driving skill, something else is required—something essential.

## Courage

When a driver steps into a racecar enough times, he knows he is eventually going to crash. That's a rule—not a maybe.

People really have died doing this. That's a fact.

Sometimes, a driver has no control whether he is going to crash or not. That's also a fact. When a car goes out of control at a superspeedway race, it's not uncommon for a dozen or more cars to be part of the crash. There's no choice in the matter. Drivers know all of the risks before they ever step into a car and yet they get in willingly.

Courage? Yes, in very large amounts. But there is more to it than a willingness to take risks.

## Mental Toughness

In 1999 at a night race in August at Bristol Motor Speedway, Dale Earnhardt Sr. spun out Terry Labonte on the last lap and then said, "I didn't mean to wreck him. I just wanted to rattle his cage."

Cages get rattled a lot in NASCAR and drivers have to be able to take it. Earnhardt, who died tragically at Daytona in 2001, had the nickname, The Intimidator. But he is not the last of the NASCAR intimidators. The style lives on. He just happened to be the best ever.

*(Courtesy of Mark Hawkins.)*

*Dale Earnhardt explained this crash of Terry Labonte on the last lap at Bristol in August, 1999 this way: "I didn't mean to wreck him. I just wanted to rattle his cage."*

All drivers know that at any time on a racetrack they can be an intimidator, or the one being challenged. It's a long race and emotions come

*A full house and a prime time audience for the Daytona 500.*

*Dale Earnhardt Jr. leads the field at the short track in Martinsville.*

*Juan Pablo Montoya describes his car's handling to his crew chief.*

*Tony Stewart, Dale Earnhardt Jr., and a TV crew enjoy a parade lap at Martinsville.*

*Part of the patriotic pre-race show at Bristol.*

*Sunset at Lowes Motor Speedway.*

*The Red Army of Dale Earnhardt Jr. cheers on their man at Talladega.*

*Even the most popular driver can have a bad day.*

*On a superspeedway, the crashes can be big …*

*… as Kyle Busch can attest. He walked away from this crash.*

This is what restrictor plate racing is all about.

Four tires, 22 gallons of gas, and a clean windshield in 14 seconds.

It takes a lot of people to win a trophy.

*Stuff happens. In NASCAR, you deal with it.*

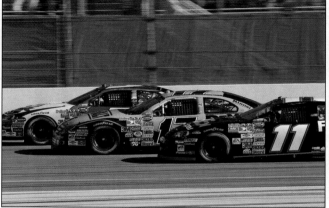

*Three wide at 191 mph.*

*#47 Jon Wood is bent, battered, and on fire at Bristol.*

into play as the race progresses. Anyone who has ever driven to the grocery store has felt a bit of rage come on from time to time when someone cuts in front or does something stupid on the road. That's how it is in a race too—only the stakes are a bit higher than a possible dented fender.

So a driver has to deal with 42 other drivers trying to establish their "turf" in these fast-moving conditions. In this, the driver must be mentally tough enough to simply deal with the conditions and not let his emotions get the best of him.

An intimidator intimidates because he can. A good driver doesn't let his cage get rattled. He stays calm. The best drivers are the calmest, with steady heartbeats and little emotion in their voice.

 **Awesome!**

Drivers have long memories, and all drivers know that. If one driver causes a crash, another driver will most likely respond in kind—but it may not be for a few races. Nevertheless, nothing that happens on a racetrack is forgotten and very little is forgiven. It's an ongoing drama.

But things happen, of course, and every driver is human. Yet some deal with things better than others or know when to let emotions take charge and when to hold them back and let logic dictate his actions. After all, it's a long race.

# Endurance

Think of it as driving from Cleveland to New York ... or New Orleans to Dallas. Endurance? Try doing that without a bathroom break or one opportunity to stretch or rest your mind.

There are no relaxing moments for a NASCAR driver. The concentration requires full-time, jumping-synapse reactions—at the very top of the game for hours ... almost four hours.

At any moment, something could happen so don't blink. At any moment for a whole bunch of moments that become minutes and then hours some wild crash could happen and the driver, on edge always, must endure. Enduring is, in fact, what he does—an essential part of the job description.

And speaking of job description, there is more to the job of driver than driving. Much of this other work requires endurance as well.

# The Showman—Doing the Sponsor's Work

"My Widgets Inc. Edsal drove great today and I'm going to celebrate by drinking a can of delicious Sponsor Soda."

Something like this is usually the first sentence uttered by a winner of a Sprint Cup Race. And the reason is obvious—racing costs a lot of money and the sponsor pays the bills. A modern NASCAR driver is as good at dropping the sponsor's name into almost any public sentence as he is at handling a racecar—because he has to be.

But doing the sponsor's work involves a lot more than simply using the name whenever the driver is interviewed. It also involves more than appearing in a commercial. The driver is a drawing card for many events for the sponsor and is expected to attend and to be on his best and most charismatic behavior. And even though he may have to tell the same story over and over, he has to tell it in a fresh and exciting way for every new audience.

*(Courtesy of Bryan Hallman.)*

*Selling for the sponsor is a big part of the job.*

The driver is an entertainer, and he makes entertainer money. A case can be made that among the many talented drivers, looks and charisma are serious criteria that owners consider. The ability to sell cannot be underestimated. A driver who is good on the track and off the track is a car owner's dream.

Even on the track the sponsor is important, and the pressures can actually affect the race.

Each sponsor is given a Sponsors Report that tells the exact amount of in-focus airtime their logo (on a car) received and the number of verbal references the company name is given during the broadcast of a race. This is then compared to the cost of a commercial for the same amount of time. And that's how sponsors justify sponsoring a car.

And that's another reason why drivers feel pressure to lead a race—at least for a while. The camera focuses on the leader, and that shows up in the Sponsors Report.

# The Celebrity in a Glass House

As NASCAR has grown into a huge sport, the 43 drivers in any given race are much more than simply drivers—and the handful at the top are bona fide American celebrities. A lot of that celebrity is very good.

For one thing, the money at the top is celebrity big—into the millions of dollars, even the many millions. And certainly, the lifestyle of fame isn't completely bad. There is much about all the adoration and perks of being a top driver that almost any human would want.

But fame always comes with a price and the modern NASCAR driver is paying that price more than any of his predecessors. Of course, he is paid more in cash and adoration, too.

**Awesome!**

The south shore of Lake Norman in North Carolina is where many NASCAR drivers have homes—er, mansions. It's also home to NBA and NFL stars. The lake, with 500 miles of shoreline, is where drivers often go for refuge.

But the exposure is double-edged because that is the nature of modern celebrity. The NASCAR driver is no longer immune. In the two-month off-season especially, NASCAR reporting is a soap opera about a million things that aren't racing.

In 2007, one driver's wife was having a baby. Another was embroiled in an ownership dispute with his stepmother. It's great gossipy stuff and fans are begged to wonder how it will affect them on the track. Maybe these are fair questions or maybe they aren't—but they exist and in the future the spotlight will only get brighter.

Sometimes drivers ask for their celebrity—by appearing on talk shows and in commercials—as much as have it thrust upon them. Just as in race strategy (see Chapter 7), there are a million organic factors that play into celebrity and the best of the best are able to adjust and remain calm amidst the 200-miles-per-hour hype of peaks and valleys.

# Champion Drivers and Cars

At the end, someone wins. When someone wins a lot (see Chapter 4) he is the champion.

Here is a list of champions at the top level (see Chapter 4) of NASCAR since 1949, when champions were crowned. Remember (see Chapter 2) the name of the championship has changed through the years.

| YEAR | DRIVER | CAR | CHAMPIONSHIP |
|------|--------|-----|--------------|
| 1949 | Red Byron | Oldsmobile | Strictly Stock |
| 1950 | Bill Rexford | Oldsmobile | Grand National |
| 1951 | Herb Thomas | Hudson | Grand National |
| 1952 | Tim Flock | Hudson | Grand National |
| 1953 | Herb Thomas | Hudson | Grand National |
| 1954 | Lee Petty | Chrysler | Grand National |
| 1955 | Tim Flock | Chrysler | Grand National |
| 1956 | Buck Baker | Chrysler | Grand National |
| 1957 | Buck Baker | Chevrolet | Grand National |
| 1958 | Lee Petty | Oldsmobile | Grand National |
| 1959 | Lee Petty | Plymouth | Grand National |
| 1960 | Rex White | Chevrolet | Grand National |

| YEAR | DRIVER | CAR | CHAMPIONSHIP |
|------|--------|-----|--------------|
| 1961 | Ned Jarrett | Chevrolet | Grand National |
| 1962 | Joe Weatherly | Pontiac | Grand National |
| 1963 | Joe Weatherly | Pontiac | Grand National |
| 1964 | Richard Petty | Plymouth | Grand National |
| 1965 | Ned Jarrett | Ford | Grand National |
| 1966 | David Pearson | Dodge | Grand National |
| 1967 | Richard Petty | Plymouth | Grand National |
| 1968 | David Pearson | Ford | Grand National |
| 1969 | David Pearson | Ford | Grand National |
| 1970 | Bobby Isaac | Dodge | Grand National |
| 1971 | Richard Petty | Plymouth | Grand National |
| 1972 | Richard Petty | Plymouth | Winston Cup |
| 1973 | Benny Parsons | Chevrolet | Winston Cup |
| 1974 | Richard Petty | Dodge | Winston Cup |
| 1975 | Richard Petty | Dodge | Winston Cup |
| 1976 | Cale Yarborough | Chevrolet | Winston Cup |
| 1977 | Cale Yarborough | Chevrolet | Winston Cup |
| 1978 | Cale Yarborough | Oldsmobile | Winston Cup |
| 1979 | Richard Petty | Chevrolet | Winston Cup |
| 1980 | Dale Earnhardt | Chevrolet | Winston Cup |
| 1981 | Darrell Waltrip | Buick | Winston Cup |
| 1982 | Darrell Waltrip | Buick | Winston Cup |
| 1983 | Bobby Allison | Buick | Winston Cup |
| 1984 | Terry Labonte | Chevrolet | Winston Cup |
| 1985 | Darrell Waltrip | Chevrolet | Winston Cup |
| 1986 | Dale Earnhardt | Chevrolet | Winston Cup |
| 1987 | Dale Earnhardt | Chevrolet | Winston Cup |
| 1988 | Bill Elliott | Ford | Winston Cup |
| 1989 | Rusty Wallace | Pontiac | Winston Cup |
| 1990 | Dale Earnhardt | Chevrolet | Winston Cup |
| 1991 | Dale Earnhardt | Chevrolet | Winston Cup |
| 1992 | Alan Kulwicki | Ford | Winston Cup |

*continues*

*continued*

| YEAR | DRIVER | CAR | CHAMPIONSHIP |
|------|--------|-----|--------------|
| 1993 | Dale Earnhardt | Chevrolet | Winston Cup |
| 1994 | Dale Earnhardt | Chevrolet | Winston Cup |
| 1995 | Jeff Gordon | Chevrolet | Winston Cup |
| 1996 | Terry Labonte | Chevrolet | Winston Cup |
| 1997 | Jeff Gordon | Chevrolet | Winston Cup |
| 1998 | Jeff Gordon | Chevrolet | Winston Cup |
| 1999 | Dale Jarrett | Ford | Winston Cup |
| 2000 | Bobby Labonte | Pontiac | Winston Cup |
| 2001 | Jeff Gordon | Chevrolet | Winston Cup |
| 2002 | Tony Stewart | Pontiac | Winston Cup |
| 2003 | Matt Kenseth | Ford | Winston Cup |
| 2004 | Kurt Busch | Ford | Nextel Cup |
| 2005 | Tony Stewart | Chevrolet | Nextel Cup |
| 2006 | Jimmie Johnson | Chevrolet | Nextel Cup |

## The Least You Need to Know

◆ A NASCAR driver is a celebrity with many jobs beyond driving the car.

◆ On the race track, drivers need driving skill, courage, mental toughness, and endurance.

◆ Drivers use the sponsor's name in every interview.

◆ Drivers' private lives are up for examination in modern celebrity culture.

# 9

# Thirteen Seconds of Organized Chaos—the Pit Crew

## In This Chapter

- ◆ The three phases of evolution of a NASCAR pit crew
- ◆ The pit wall and who goes over it
- ◆ The people behind the wall
- ◆ The choreography of a pit stop

Thirteen seconds of intense manual labor by the pit crew can decide whether a driver wins a four-hour race.

The speed of the pit crew determines track position out of the pit and track position is critical. The job of the pit crew is to give the best 13 (or less!) seconds possible and then wait and be ready for the next time they are called into action.

The evolution of the pit crew—from the days of an uncle or a brother or a best friend helping change tires to the modern days of high-paid professional athletes—is just another example of the over-all evolution of the sport from a good-old-boys-helping-a-pal way of doing things into a corporate systems-oriented culture. Competition as well as the rules leveling the competition made the transformation of pit crews necessary.

This is a chapter about the pit crew and the 13 seconds of organized chaos that can make or break a team's chances to win. It will begin by covering the evolution of the pit crew and then it will discuss the basics of a modern pit crew including the jobs over the wall, and the jobs not over the wall. Finally, this chapter will describe the choreography of a standard pit stop.

# The Three Historical Phases of the NASCAR Pit Crew

The pit crew has gone through three phases and though each team has developed a bit differently, the progression has been pretty clear. It has also been, as most of NASCAR is, a game of follow the leader.

◆ When NASCAR first began (see Chapter 2), drivers would show up at the track, often with their own car, and then just go racing. Maybe an uncle or a brother came along to help when the driver inevitably needed to stop. As often as not, the driver would help change his own tires. The pit stop wasn't important in a 500-mile race in which the differences in cars was often huge—as in multiple-laps difference.

◆ In the second phase, mechanics began traveling with the team— along with a crew chief and an engine specialist. And then in the 1960s, Leonard Wood of Wood Brothers Racing, car owners since 1950, was the first to organize a pit stop into a series of specific movements and tasks. This revolutionized the sport and transformed the pit stop into a competitive part of the sport—recognized as a way to give a driver an edge. The Wood Brothers had such impressive pit stops on the NASCAR circuit that they were brought in by Ford Motor Company to pit its car driven by Jim Clark in the 1965 Indianapolis 500. Clark won the race and the Wood Brothers' fame grew larger.

◆ In 1992, Andy Papathanassiou, a Stanford graduate with a Master's in organizational behavior was hired by owner Rick Hendrick and crew chief Ray Evernham to coach Jeff Gordon's pit crew. Recognized as the godfather of the modern pit crew, "Andy Papa," as he is known, helped Gordon win championships in the mid-1990s. His training techniques and the revolution of bringing athletes into the pit box lowered average pit times by 5 seconds. Other car owners soon followed suit, and now top pit crewmembers make more than $100,000 a year. The pit crew are now autograph-signing TV celebrity-athletes who train accordingly.

# Pit Basics

The pit stall is an all-purpose NASCAR garage at a racetrack. Okay— the truth is that it is a parking space.

Some tracks have stalls that are bigger than those at other tracks. For instance, a pit stall at California Motor Speedway is 1.5 times bigger than that at Bristol Motor Speedway.

But essentially, spaces are lined up in a stretch just off the racetrack called pit road. Each pit road is configured differently. Drivers get to choose which space to pit in based on their qualifying time (see Chapter 4). And then the car pulls in—moving from right to left as seen from the view of the crew—and stops while work is quickly done so the driver can get back on the track.

At the pit, there are two groups of people waiting. There is a group of seven—sometimes eight—who are allowed over the wall. And then there are others—an unspecified number but not too many—who are not over the wall.

Wait—wall? Yes, there is a two-foot-high, 10-inch-wide, cinderblock brick wall separating pit road from the infield. During a race, only seven—later in the race it is eight—crewmembers can go over the wall and work on the car.

Other crewmembers work—and think—behind the wall. In addition, standing on a huge tool chest called a pit box is a crew chief running everything like a combination of symphony conductor, Broadway director, and NFL coach—with more than a bit of mechanic/engineer thrown in.

# Seven (Sometimes Eight) Over the Wall

Seven crewmembers are allowed over the wall to work on the car during a pit stop.

After the first pit stop—when NASCAR decides—an eighth crewmember is allowed over the wall to bring food or drink to the driver. This eighth crewmember is limited to what he can do—clean the windshield (more later), or help the driver.

The other seven over-the-wall crewmembers have very individual jobs with specialized roles. They can do many things but their specific jobs are:

◆ **Jack Man**—He jacks up the car using a special aluminum jack that raises the car 8-$^1/_2$ inches in one pump. He jacks up both sides of the car—right side and then left side—so that the tire changers can change the tires. He needs tremendous hand-eye coordination, speed, and strength.

◆ **Front Tire Changer**—He changes the front tires on both sides of the car. The most important part of his job is wielding the compressed-air gun that loosens and tightens the lug nuts. He must be precise in his actions.

**Awesome!**

New lug nuts are attached to the wheel with a weather stripping adhesive so that when the tire is put on, the lug nuts simply need to be tightened. In the old days of NASCAR, a tire changer carried his extra lug nuts in his mouth.

◆ **Rear Tire Changer**—He changes the rear tires on both sides of the car. The most important part of his job is wielding the compressed-air gun that loosens and tightens the lug nuts. He must be precise in his actions.

◆ **Front Tire Carrier**—He carries the tires for the front tire changer. He also lines up and mounts the tire onto the car so the front tire changer can tighten the lug nuts.

He must be especially strong to carry a 70-pound tire and he needs great hand-eye coordination to line up the tire.

◆ **Rear Tire Carrier**—He carries the tires for the rear tire changer. He also lines up and mounts the tire onto the car so the rear tire changer can tighten the lug nuts. He must be especially strong to carry a 70-pound tire and he needs great hand-eye coordination to line up the tire.

◆ **Gas Man**—He puts gas in the car. He uses a special 11-gallon fuel can with a special valve that allows the fuel to enter the car quickly by the force of gravity.

◆ **Catch Can Man**—He uses a special container—a catch can—to catch overflow fuel from when the car is being filled.

## Safety

Pit road is a dangerous place. The greatest danger, though not the only one, faced by pit crew is getting hit by a car. They are running around within inches of their own driver's car and just a few feet from the pit box (one on each end of their own car) of another driver.

Cars are coming down pit row at speeds ranging between 35 and 55 mph, depending on the track, plenty fast enough speed to hurt a pedestrian. Of course, these are not ordinary pedestrians and this is no ordinary street. Pit crewmembers actually used to wear just t-shirts and shorts but those days are long gone. Now they wear full fire suits, helmets, kneepads, and fire-retardant gloves.

A big worry is the equipment, especially hoses for the air guns, can sometimes get caught under or on a car. And other drivers are not always perfectly understanding of the rights of pedestrians who might be standing in the way of their chance to win. It is a dangerous place, requiring a safety dance of courage, instincts, and athleticism.

## Experience and Background

College and even professional athletes are now recruited. Mechanical skill is not needed in the pit crew since the tasks are straightforward.

Speed and dexterity are needed. So is strength. Most important is the mental ability to focus and block out the dangerous situation, the noise of the crowd and cars, and the pressure of an intense situation. All the classic athletic skills found in sports such as football and baseball are perfect for the modern pit crew.

## Pay

The pay varies wildly. Top pit athletes can, with bonuses for good performance, make more than $100,000 year. Others, just getting started, will actually volunteer for a lower level team that cannot afford to pay top dollar to their pit crew.

Every organization is different. Some are big, well-funded, multi-car teams with the ability and means to employ and train the very best pit athletes. Although all organizations understand the need for a top-flight pit crew, not all can afford them.

**Awesome!**

Pit crewmembers often learn their trade at Pit Crew U.—an entity of Pit Instruction & Training (PIT) located in Mooresville, NC. PIT trains professional crewmembers as well as "wannabes." PIT also teaches the same skills to corporations looking to improve teamwork and speed in any areas. For more information, see www.pit-now.com

Even those crewmembers that get paid may be compensated differently from team to team. Some are actually full-time athletes training and working as pit crew—and that's it.

Other teams bring the pit crew into their team's race shop during the week to perform various mechanical tasks on and around the car. This part-time garage work would factor into their overall pay as an employee of the team.

Others might have a full-time job doing something completely different—doctor, lawyer, truck driver—and then they train with the crew a few times a week.

And others really do volunteer with the hope of landing a paying gig somewhere else. Sometimes, if these less experienced volunteers are working on a car that is performing better than expected on the race-track, the volunteers may get fired mid-race and replaced by more experienced professionals who can help the driver's chance to win. Yes, crewmembers, even paid crewmembers, can be fired mid-race if they are not performing well.

## Training

Training is an essential part of the job in order to maintain and improve performance. Big teams even employ several coaches to train their pit athletes—including a pit crew coordinator for pit stop skills and a conditioning coordinator to keep the crew in shape. There are really three kinds of training for pit crews:

- ◆ **Physical conditioning**—Although the burst required is short—13 or 14 seconds—it is intense, like an NFL or baseball play. Quick, intense action requires training to be the best. Since each job is specialized, the training is slightly different but essentially all crewmembers work on speed, endurance (yes, it is short bursts, but it is a long day and the race season—see Chapter 4—is one of the longest in all of sports), agility, and flexibility.

- ◆ **On-the-car training**—Muscle memory is a key part of getting to be the best. The only way to train the muscles is to, well, train the muscles repetitively. In order, for instance, for a tire changer to hit the lug nuts perfectly and consistently, he must practice.

- ◆ **Film/prep work**—A pit stop is choreographed and the action is filmed. Each step, each movement, is precise in order to save time. And each pit stop is then analyzed much like an NFL play is ana-lyzed in the film room. In addition, since each track and pit stalls are different, teams must prepare ahead of time for what to expect.

## Those Not (Usually) Over the Wall

An unspecified number of people, determined by the funding of the team, are with the crew behind the wall in order to help out. Often mechanics and engineers, they are close enough to see the car when it pulls up and they may be called on to don a fire suit and helmet later in the race if the car needs extensive repairs.

There are a few specific jobs:

- The eighth over-the-wall crewmember is not always over the wall. When he does go over the wall, he is only allowed to bring food or drink to the driver or to clean the windshield.

---

**Awesome!** _____

Cleaning the windshield involves tearing a thin plastic sheet off. This sheet, during the race, collects tire dust and dirt, so when it is pulled off the dirt is gone. The special, unbreakable Lexan windshield is coated with a few sheets that can be pulled off during the race. That way the expensive windshield itself doesn't get damaged.

---

- The sign man holds a long pole with a sign on it showing the driver exactly where to stop so the crew can come out and work on the car. The sign is usually a special color, the driver's number, or a corporate logo—something easy to spot among 42 other signs.

- The crew chief stands on a pit box near the pit stall. He wears a radio headset and can communicate with the driver, the crew, and the spotter (see Chapter 7). The crew chief interprets what the driver wants (see Chapters 7 and 8) and then places an order with the pit crew so that they know exactly what to do and are prepared to do it when the driver pulls up. Most modern crew chiefs have engineering backgrounds and some have served on crews themselves.

# Inside the Pit Considerations

As you learned in Chapter 7, speed by the pit crew determines track position coming off of pit road. Since it is so difficult to pass on the racetrack, losing a few spots because of a slow tire change can be fatal to a team's chances to win.

The cars are so close in modern NASCAR that the pit stop has become a key difference between winning and losing. Although the strategy of what to do was covered in Chapter 7, there is yet another consideration—where to do it and who to have as pit row neighbors.

Pit stalls are chosen in order of qualifying, and the best qualifiers clearly select the best spots—usually the closest to the exit of pit row. But there is even more to it. Pitting near a teammate makes the most sense because a car owned by the same owner will most likely be respectful of the neighboring crew. Pitting further away from a competitor who is "aggressive" getting into and out of their pit stall can save a crewmember from injury. And that can make a difference.

The crew itself has to live vicariously through the driver—just like his fans—until it is their show time. And then when it is, they must be able to go from a mode of boredom and waiting into a mode of frantic organization that is competitively faster than other teams. And then it's over, and they wait to do it again.

One more word about pit stops—the last one is the most important. Of course, all the crews know the same thing and often the entire race strategy (see Chapter 7) is contingent on doing the perfect final pit stop at the right time. For the pit crew, that final pit stop is crunch time—the same as when the ball is in the shooter's hands in the final seconds of a basketball game, or a baseball player at bat in the bottom of the ninth inning.

# The Choreography of a Pit Stop

Every movement in the choreography of a typical four-tire, fuel-up pit stop is planned. But first, think about what the crew has been doing—waiting.

Remember, before all of this happens, the crew has been sitting and watching and cheering and, well, the saying is *long stretches of boredom separated by moments of sheer terror.* They've been waiting. And waiting. They are in the loop about the strategy and they are prepared but they have been—what's that word—waiting. And waiting. Maybe they've been stretching or talking or getting equipment ready but for the most part they've been doing one thing—waiting. Waiting—watching and waiting.

And then ... the moment.

*(Courtesy of Bryan Haltman.)*

*A pit stop is a rush.*

He's on his way and everything—everything—is choreographed except for the adrenalin. Like the greatest rock guitar chord ever hit, it happens in an instant. The car pulls in, stops, the tires are changed and the car is fueled and then it is gone. Poof. Over like that.

But within that blink of time—and it appears to happen in an instant—is an intricate dance of man and machine (and fuel can, and so on) that is planned and practiced and perfected to the point of chasing tenths and even hundredths of a second.

## The Car Enters the Pit

The car enters the pit from the right of the crewmembers—and the crewmembers wait. The first action can be taken by the jack man, the front tire changer, and the front tire carrier, who are allowed to go over the wall as soon as the front of their car passes the front line of the pit behind their pit.

By running in front of a racecar, the crew is showing incredible trust in the driver, who is also showing incredible trust in his crew not to stop in the wrong place. At this point, the dance has begun.

Three people run in front of the car while the sign man holds a sign so that the driver knows where to stop. And all other teams are doing this at the same time.

## The Right Side of the Car

As soon as the car comes to a stop, the jack man is lining up the jack plate on his jack, which is about the size of a CD and fits at a certain spot, a metal rod sticking out of each side of the bottom of the car, facing toward the ground. This rod, about the diameter of a quarter, is called the jack peg.

At the same time, the front wheel changer and front wheel carrier are getting in position to briskly and meticulously attack the lug nuts on the right front tire.

When the car stops, the rear tire changer and rear tire carrier run around the back of the car, and the rear tire changer immediately attacks the lug nuts on the rear tire. This is when the dance becomes intricate.

The front tire changer, having removed all the lug nuts, puts down his gun and physically pulls the tire off of the car. The front tire carrier then puts the tire on after first *indexing the tire.*

The front tire carrier then holds the tire in place while the front tire changer tightens the first two lug nuts. Then the front tire carrier grabs the old tire and carries it to a support person over the wall, who then gives him a new tire for the left side.

**Awesome!**

The car is not allowed to run over or under any piece of equipment as it is entering or leaving the pit. It cannot leave any piece of equipment attached to the car. The crew must be extra careful to have all the equipment and tires on the inside (left half) of the car when it leaves the pit area.

**Pit Stop!**

**Indexing a tire** is what a tire carrier does to line up the lug nut holes with the lug nuts. He visually indexes it to find exactly where everything is so he can slip the tire on smoothly on the first try.

Meanwhile, the rear tire workers are a little behind because they had to wait for the car to stop before they could run out and begin their work. And so the timing becomes even more intricate.

As soon as the rear tire changer has removed the lug nuts, he—unlike the front tire changer—does not put down his gun. Instead, in order to help out and save precious time, the jack man steps over and removes the tire. Then he steps around the rear of the car and rolls it to the support team waiting behind the wall.

At this time, the rear tire carrier indexes and mounts the tire while the rear tire changer begins to tighten the lug nuts. At that exact moment, the jack man drops the car and begins the dash to the other side. His help of the rear tire changer is just enough to get the two tire changers in synch for their work on the left side.

## The Left Side of the Car

In fact, the two tire changers are faster than the jack man around to the left side of the car. They are in position to take the lug nuts off by the time the jack is under the left side of the car.

When the jack man pumps the car up, the tire changers have all five lug nuts off already. (The left side needs a little extra jacking—a pump and a bump—because it carries the driver and extra weight to make it turn left easier.)

Then the tire changers remove the tires, the tire carriers index and mount the tires, and the tire changers attach the five lug nuts.

As soon as the jack man sees the gun come out of the tires—it's his visual cue—he drops the car. The driver is already spinning the tires so the car hits the ground running—all in about 13 seconds.

## A Word About the Fuel

As soon as the car stops, the gas man begins dumping the special 11-gallon container of fuel, commonly called a "dump can," into the rear left of the car while the catch can man is positioned behind the rear bumper, almost immediately behind the driver.

When the right-to-left shift begins by the jack man, tire changers, and tire carriers, the rear tire changer must run around the catch can man but in between the gas man and the car.

Often, a car will take more fuel than one dump can hold. This means the gas man will remove his empty can from the car, hand it over the wall, and get another can of fuel.

# The Officials Are Watching

The entire time of the pit stop, a NASCAR official, in a fire suit and helmet, is watching carefully as a reminder that no cheating is allowed. He is also watching especially to be sure all five lug nuts are on each wheel.

Sometimes if one car pits next to an empty stall, the neighboring official will look in on the pit stop.

## The Least You Need to Know

◆ Pit stops are crucial to chances for victory.

◆ A NASCAR pit crew has evolved from relatives and friends helping out into a crew of highly paid, well-trained professional athletes.

◆ Staying alert during long waits is important.

◆ Seven go over the pit wall to change tires and add fuel.

◆ The choreography of a pit stop is intricate and practiced.

# Chapter 10

# A Money Tree with a Logo—the Business of NASCAR

## In This Chapter

- ◆ A look at the costs to race
- ◆ A description of who owns what
- ◆ Why sponsorship works
- ◆ An examination of the stickers on the car
- ◆ A glimpse into the future

The sport of NASCAR is big business—and that means big money. Money doesn't just buy the gasoline. Money, in many ways, is the figurative gasoline that makes the entire expensive sport go. Follow the leader? Follow the money.

According to *Parade* Magazine's annual report of what people earn (April 18, 2007 issue) Nextel Cup champion Jimmie Johnson earned $15.8 million in 2006. His face appeared on the cover of the magazine between the photo of a minister who earned $9,000 and a postal carrier who earned $49,200.

What does it mean? It means that Jimmie Johnson is a top-level professional athlete/entertainer and paid accordingly. But Jimmie Johnson's very public pay is just one branch of a complex money tree. NASCAR is big business.

This is a chapter about the many aspects of the business of NASCAR. It will discuss the importance of money: where it comes in, where it goes out, and in general who gets what. It will cover details such as the cost to participate, ownership of NASCAR, racetracks, and cars; as well as sponsorship, souvenirs, television, and what the future holds. So let's follow the money.

# An Expensive Sport

Racing is expensive. A car and a 100-person team behind it can cost $15 million to $20 million a year.

These costs include multiple copies of the car (engineered slightly differently for different racetracks), plus an engine and labor for each car. In addition, there are costs for an engine program, travel, tires, and overhead such as facilities and the like.

The best teams own more than one car, and this allows them to share some research, employees, and space. But in the end, it's not about saving money. It's about making money. And if you want to make bunch of money, it's always best to start with a bunch of money.

# Who Owns What in NASCAR's World?

NASCAR is a private company, started by Bill France Sr. (see Chapter 2), and still owned by the France family.

International Speedway Corporation (ISC) is a publicly traded company listed on the NASDAQ stock exchange. It owns 12 racetracks hosting Sprint Cup races. The France family owns the majority of voting stock in ISC. The fact that the France family owns NASCAR and the majority of ISC, which hosts NASCAR races, has brought charges of conflict of interest against the family as well as antitrust lawsuits (some still pending) from other track owners trying to get a NASCAR race.

Speedway Motorsports Inc. (SMI), owned by Bruton Smith, owns six racetracks on the cup circuit. SMI owns the second most racetracks hosting cup races. No one else owns more than one racetrack.

There are a few single car owners in the sport but the old days of an owner/driver are almost at an end. The sport is almost too expensive for an individual car to compete. The most successful drivers in recent years have come from teams where the owner owns multiple cars.

Here is an unofficial list of the car owners in NASCAR and the car manufacturers associated with each.

| Car Owner | Manufacturer |
| --- | --- |
| BAM Racing | Dodge |
| Bill Davis Racing | Toyota |
| Chip Ganassi Racing | Dodge |
| Dale Earnhardt Inc. | Chevrolet |
| Evernham Motorsports | Dodge |
| Haas CNC Racing | Chevrolet |
| Hendrick Motorsports | Chevrolet |
| Joe Gibbs Racing | Chevrolet |
| Michael Waltrip Racing | Toyota |
| Morgan-McClure Motorsports | Chevrolet |
| Penske Racing | Dodge |
| Petty Racing | Dodge |
| Richard Childress Racing | Chevrolet |
| Robert Yates | Ford |
| Roush Fenway Racing | Ford |
| Wood Brothers Racing | Ford |

# Corporate America's Partner

Corporate America has a love affair with NASCAR, which encourages and nourishes that love every second of every day. The relationship is, as experts in corporate jargon like to say, a win-win situation.

This situation exists in that magical crossroads where supply—in this case the supply of rabid, loyal fans—meets demand, which is a demand to cash in on that loyalty. This creates a perfect, pressure-filled, high-profile capitalistic model that is incredibly complex yet elementary.

# The "Official" Answer—Why Do They Invest in NASCAR?

But why invest in NASCAR? Begin with this simple, obvious truth: the cars are rolling billboards that are on a highly rated television show.

Unlike the other major stick and ball sports, which have created their own team logos, fans of NASCAR drivers find themselves rooting, in part, for a corporation. If you are a corporation, can it get any better than that? The truth is that it probably can't.

Seventy-five million people identify themselves as NASCAR fans and people who are NASCAR fans have proven to have extra brand loyalty. They have loyalty to their brand of car and to the sponsor of their favorite driver. But there is more to it than that.

Fans have proven loyal to "the official" *everything* of NASCAR—and that's why there is so much that is, well, official. It costs big money to be the official anything of NASCAR but the benefit is officially tremendous. If the benefits weren't great, corporate America wouldn't keep investing.

# Sponsorship Money

Logos on the car are only one branch of the money tree. In fact, the growing, evolving money tree that is the world of NASCAR has more branches than most fans can name and most of those branches have branches ...

And the tangle of varied corporate interests that tangentially or directly affect the race team has grown. So let's start with the obvious: sponsorship. Sponsorship is much broader than advertising, and in NASCAR sponsorship falls into three main categories.

# NASCAR in General

NASCAR is a licensing body. That means it sells the right to be the "official" whatever of NASCAR, which is a bragging right that pays dividends with the loyal audience.

And so while cars—you may have noticed—have sponsors (more later), so does NASCAR itself. In fact, the premier series is called the Sprint Cup. Previously it was called the Nextel Cup, however, Nextel was bought by Sprint and the series name changed in 2008. In fact, Nextel had bought the name of NASCAR's premier series for 10 years and $700 million before this name change. The series previously was called the Winston Cup.

Sprint has leveraged that name dramatically in a number of ways. The proof is in the numbers. According to a November 15, 2006, MSNBC. com story, "Sprint Nextel customers who are NASCAR fans generate 20 percent more revenue for the company than do Sprint Nextel customers who are not NASCAR fans, says the company."

Sprint is a perfect example of how sponsorship in NASCAR is not just a put-your-name-on-it-and-expect-results kind of deal. It is much more proactive.

The company has introduced a new kind of handheld technology at racetracks, called a FanView, that allows fans—for a rental price of $50 for a race to $70 for the weekend—to receive streaming live race video and audio while at the track.

Sprint, which sponsors the Sprint Cup series, used its sponsorship to get exclusive access to NASCAR fans. By bringing hardcore race fans—those at the track—closer to the action than ever, the company has most likely increased loyalty while adding the over-the-shoulder, hey-what's-that curiosity about its latest cool technology. This is classic win-win for the company and for NASCAR—plus the fans win, too.

Besides selling the names to its various racing series, and the official sponsorship deals, NASCAR also makes money through various sponsors whose decals appear on the front quarter panels of all cars (more later).

*The FanView handheld device, rented by Sprint to fans at racetracks, provides live streaming race video and audio at the track.*

*(Courtesy of Bryan Hallman.)*

## The Racetracks

The old saying is that NASCAR owns everything from the black circle in, and the racetrack owns everything outside of the black circle. Of course that's simplified, but it's a good start to your continuing education.

The racetracks and NASCAR are different. Some say not always completely different, but different enough in that the racetracks have sponsorship deals separate from NASCAR.

For instance, many races are named after a corporation—the Kobalt Tools 500; the Pepsi 400, and so on. The race name is sold to the corporation. The racetrack sells it.

In addition, sponsors of cars (keep reading) rent "hospitality tents" at racetracks, and from the racetracks, to entertain clients and fans. And that—the sponsors of the cars paying the racetracks—is one example of the gray area of sponsorship. The relationship of the sponsors to the various entities is complicated for many reasons, including that the lines between the entities themselves are sometimes murky and the corporations are interested in individual cars as well as the bigger picture.

## Team Owners

As you've most likely noticed, the cars of NASCAR have very interesting paint jobs that look a lot like corporate logos. This is because these cars cost a lot of money (more later) to run and the only way an owner can afford to compete is to partner up with a corporation that is willing to invest/gamble millions of dollars.

There are not a lot of companies with the money and willingness to invest in a NASCAR Sprint Cup car, but there are enough of them to put on a heck of a show.

### Awesome!

Racing is so expensive that some cars have revolving sponsors, maybe two or three throughout the season. In 2007, Jeff Burton began the season running in a Cingular car, but changed to Prilosec OTC on his #31 Chevrolet for the race in Texas. Interestingly, Burton won in Texas, giving lots of airtime to Prilosec OTC's logo.

The cost of investing in a car as the primary sponsor with the big logo on the hood is variable, depending on a lot of factors—especially the success of the driver. But it certainly runs several million dollars for any car, and from $15 million to $20 million for the top cars.

# What Does a Car Sponsor Get for the Money?

Sponsors get bragging rights.

The sponsor, whether sponsoring the premier series, a race, a car, or part of a car (more later), gets to associate itself with one of the most popular sports in the country. It's *"Hey, Look at us!"* And it works.

Every company that invests has learned that it works because, again, NASCAR fans are among the most loyal customers on Earth. When a company associates its name with something-NASCAR, it can then leverage that in many profitable and high-profile ways.

But because there are so many legal contractual relationships in NASCAR—owner to driver; owner to sponsor; sponsor to driver; owner to NASCAR; sponsor to NASCAR; and so on—and because the interests are often the same but sometimes varied, the rewards and perks of sponsorship are complicated.

Take the sponsor of a car, for instance. The sponsor has a contract with the car owner. The car owner has a contract with the driver. And the driver may have a separate contract with the sponsor, but more likely his contract with the car owner covers all aspects of his relationship with the sponsor.

The sponsor expects the driver to be part of the whole sponsorship deal. In many ways, a sponsor is not just sponsoring the driver's car, but it is also hiring the driver as a corporate spokesman. And the driver's job as corporate spokesman (see Chapter 8) is a huge part of his overall duties.

Yet some sponsors of cars are also the "official" whatever of NASCAR and that is different than sponsoring an individual car.

# So What's with All Those Stickers on the Car?

The car (and the driver, you may have noticed) displays more than one logo. One just happens to be bigger than all the rest—except for the actual number on the car.

But the stickers are not just slapped on in a haphazard manner. Some of it is easy to follow, some of it is a bit more variable, and some of the stickers actually have to do with prize money. That's right, if you happen to be the best car with a certain sticker on your car (all cars don't run all stickers), you will win money.

Here is a quick list at the stickers on the car and where they go:

- **Primary Sponsor.** This is the biggest corporate logo, used in a number of places, and is the logo of the company the driver always refers to when he talks of his car. This logo goes on the hood, the upper rear quarter panel, the TV panel on the rear of the car, and is seen on the in-car camera. This could cost between $10 million and $20 million.

- **The Car Number.** This big number goes on the door panels, the roof, the right rear brake light, and the right front headlight.

- **Manufacturer Logo.** Lower hood, both front and rear bumpers.

- **Mandatory Signs.** The fuel supplier, Sunoco, has a logo on the side of the car in front of the front tire and the tire supplier, Goodyear, has a logo on the side of the car above the front tire.

**Awesome!**

Carl Kiekhaefer, who owned Mercury outboard engines, was the first non-manufacturer to sponsor a car. In the mid-1950s, he put the logo of his business on a fast Chrysler 300 and hired the best drivers, including legendary Tim Flock. Fans, Kiekhaefer reasoned, always noticed the best cars.

- **Major Associate Sponsor.** On top of what would be the trunk, behind rear window. This is often the major sponsor of a teammate, or one of two or three revolving major sponsors.

- **Associate Sponsors.** These small logos may be on many locations on the car, including the lower rear quarter panel, the front of the rear wheel, between the side door number and the rear wheel, and behind the front side window. These are sponsors of the car that pay team owners.

- **Contingency Sponsors.** These small logos appear on the front quarter panel of any car that chooses to run them. Often, companies pay NASCAR for running the logo and also award a prize to the team running the logo that finishes first. Smaller teams tend to run the most of these logos.

# Sometimes They Even Sponsor Individual Laps

Sponsors try to get their way into a NASCAR program, and on television, any way they can. There are even occasional sponsorships of individual laps.

Years ago at certain racetracks, local individuals such as Mr. Jones or Mrs. Smith would sponsor a lap just to get their name in the program.

# TV Money

In addition to all the sponsorship money coming into NASCAR, television revenue is another thick branch on the money tree.

NASCAR in 2007 began the first year of an eight-year television contract with Fox, ESPN/ABC, TNT, and SPEED for rights to show races of their various series, showcasing the Sprint Cup and Busch series. According to *The New York Times*, April 15, 2007, the contract is worth $4.5 billion, or $560 million a year.

**Awesome!**

NASCAR is such big business that it qualifies for academic study. Dr. Jon Ackley and Dr. Michael Pitts have created a class about the business of NASCAR at Virginia Commonwealth University called "From Dirt Tracks to Madison Avenue." They have also created a blog called, "The View From Here, The Business of NASCAR," which can be found at http://blog.vcu.edu/nascar/.

NASCAR is a brilliant business model. It convinced television networks to pay for the right to broadcast its product, and it convinced sponsors to pay to be on that television show. And then, because of the television popularity, this exposure has led to more even more deals in things such as souvenirs and collectibles and marketing of the NASCAR name.

# Other NASCAR Business Branches

Besides the three top series (see Chapter 3), NASCAR also sanctions races at smaller racetracks, and the track pays NASCAR to stage an event. Each year, NASCAR sanctions approximately 1,500 races at about 100 tracks in 38 states.

In addition, NASCAR.com, the official website of NASCAR, is produced by Turner Sports Interactive, which holds exclusive interactive rights. The site sells advertisements and offers exclusive free as well as paid content.

As a refresher, the France family owns NASCAR. Plus, the France family is the majority stockholder in International Speedway Corporation, which owns 12 racetracks hosting Sprint Cup events. But ISC is involved in much more than just the operation of racetracks. The corporation also owns:

◆ Daytona USA, "The Official Attraction of NASCAR," is an interactive motorsports attraction adjacent to Daytona International Speedway in Daytona Beach, Florida.

◆ Motorsports Radio Network (MRN), the largest independent sports radio network in the United States.

◆ Americrown Service Corporation, which provides catering, food and beverage concessions, and merchandise sales.

◆ Motorsports International, which produces and markets motorsports-related merchandise.

# One More Visit to the Racetracks

There are only 36 races a year in the Sprint Cup season. Some racetracks host two races a year, while some big racetracks that have been built hoping to lure a cup race have not been able to land one.

As NASCAR has grown, the demand for races at new racetracks in new regions has grown. The issue of placing races is complicated for a number of reasons and yet the simplest reason is really simple: every time a race is added at one racetrack, one must be taken away from another one.

> **Awesome!**
>
> NASCAR loses tradition when it moves a race. A profound example is the loss of the Southern 500, which was run from 1950 to 2003 on Labor Day weekend at Darlington Raceway. This traditional holiday weekend race is one that long-time fans particularly miss, but the date was given to California Speedway.

There are emotional, financial, and legal arguments involved in the movement of a race from an old track—most likely a traditional track from the early days of NASCAR—to a new track. Since NASCAR is the ultimate decision maker, people raise questions … sometimes in court.

Remember, NASCAR is owned by the France family, which holds controlling interest in ISC, which owns 12 tracks. That has made for some controversy and even lawsuits. Since NASCAR places races, some feel NASCAR is not objective in evaluating racetracks while NASCAR argues that ISC is a completely separate entity. The courts are busy.

# The Road Ahead; a Brief Glimpse of the Future

The growth of NASCAR has been phenomenal and the customer base is among the most loyal on Earth.

Although maybe nothing can continue to grow at the pace that NASCAR grew from the mid-1990s until now, NASCAR's evolution is far from over. Among the many issues NASCAR is currently addressing are:

- ◆ **Diversity of drivers and crew.** NASCAR has launched a diversity internship program trying to get women and minorities involved in the sport.

- ◆ **Diversity of fans.** NASCAR is reaching out to minorities and women more than ever.

- **Expansion to other countries.** NASCAR now holds Busch Series races in Canada and Mexico. NASCAR chairman Brian France recently visited China and talked of bringing NASCAR to that country.

- **Franchising.** Legendary driver Richard Petty suggested in 2007 that NASCAR teams be franchised in a model like that of professional baseball or football teams. Although no specific proposal of how franchising would work was advanced, the concept is intriguing as a way to keep traditional owners, who built NASCAR, in the sport.

But NASCAR's big question is how to evolve, as it must, and yet hold onto its tradition, as it also must. Yes, the sport of NASCAR is big business and one thing is certain: NASCAR understands the concept of going fast and staying in it for the long haul.

## The Least You Need to Know

- Racing is very expensive.

- The France family owns NASCAR. The France family also owns the majority of stock in International Speedway Corporation, which owns 12 racetracks.

- NASCAR fans are very loyal and that is a major reason why companies love to associate with the sport.

- Almost everything, including the races and the cars (and spots on cars) are sponsored by corporations. NASCAR and race teams need the money to cover their expenses, and the companies gain great advertising and customer loyalty.

- With a 36-race season, every time a race is added at one track, one must be taken away from a different track.

- NASCAR is evolving and growing.

# Chapter 11

# Glory Days—Legends and Lore

## In This Chapter

- ◆ Famous drivers, decade by decade
- ◆ Famous stories, decade by decade
- ◆ Famous NASCAR families
- ◆ Why Jeff Gordon is so controversial

Remember the time ...

The rich history of NASCAR is more than a simple timeline of events. It involves characters, crashes, famous driving families, and great duels with wild finishes that live on through legend and lore. These are reference points for fans.

When Bill France and 35 other race promoters met in 1947 (see Chapter 2) in the Ebony Lounge atop the Streamline Hotel in Daytona Beach, Florida, and formed NASCAR, they could not possibly have envisioned what was to follow. Even the visionary France couldn't have predicted some of this.

There is no way, of course, to capture every character and every dramatic event in more than a half century of NASCAR. While Chapter 2 captured some of the highlights of the chronological history that helps tell the overall story, there is a rich year-to-year/driver-to-driver story to tell as well. Of course, that would take an entire book, or more likely, a series. It seems that there's always another story to tell.

This is a chapter with some highlights of the legends and lore of NASCAR—stories that NASCAR fans just seem to know. Obviously, no list is complete. For reference, if you want to know more back-story, see Chapter 2.

This is fun information and it helps build your foundation of knowledge to be a better fan. This will give a decade-by-decade look at famous drivers and famous stories, which often overlap. It will examine the sagas of Dale Earnhardt, Darrell Waltrip, and Jeff Gordon and attempt to explain why Gordon is such a controversial figure.

# Decades of Stories and Drivers, and Even Families

NASCAR is not something that can be presented story-by-story, driver-by-driver, and decade-by-decade. Despite that fact, that is exactly the plan for this chapter.

The truth is, it all overlaps. Drivers have fascinating individual stories. They were also involved in epic events with other drivers. And some of their careers span more than one decade.

In fact, there are famous driving families such as Petty, Earnhardt, and Allison (and many others) that have had two or more family members drive. Overlap? You betcha. It all overlaps.

NASCAR is family, inside and out—with its own genealogy and history and especially famous stories passed on through the years. Yes, it's exactly like a family. There's a lot of love in NASCAR; and a couple of good tussles, too.

# 1949 to 1959

In the early days, "stock" meant stock. Period. Those were the rules and all a driver could do was weld the doors shut and live with it. All right, maybe he drank a little of the moonshine whiskey he hauled, but he lived with it and he was happy to do so. *Let's go racin'.* It's different now, but maybe it's not any different at all. Racing is racing. Isn't it?

The early drivers were *characters*—larger than life, funny, and maybe even a little wild. America was different back then and so was NASCAR.

## Great Drivers and NASCharacters

◆ **Buck Baker**—A former moonshine runner and bus driver, he won championships in 1956 and 1957 and was among the all-time winners. He later formed the Buck Baker Driving School, where Jeff Gordon was one of his students.

◆ **Robert "Red" Byron**—The winner of the first NASCAR-sanctioned race, and the winner of the first championship, Byron was a World War II veteran whose leg had to be rebuilt after being injured in the war.

◆ **Tim Flock**—He won the 1952 and 1955 championships. In 1955, Flock had a dominating year driving a Chrysler 300 for Carl Kiekhaefer. Besides his driving prowess, Flock was also a wild, funny character who once drove with a monkey he nicknamed "Jocko Flocko."

◆ **Lee Petty**—He won three championships as well as the first Daytona 500, held in 1959. One of the great drivers in early NASCAR, he was the founding member of a racing family dynasty.

◆ **Glenn "Fireball" Roberts**—He was nicknamed "Fireball" for his ability to throw a baseball but the nickname proved as memorable as his driving at the beginning of the big track era. He was known especially for dominance at Darlington. He died 37 days after he was burned in a fiery crash at the Charlotte Motor Speedway.

◆ **Herb Thomas**—He won two championships, in 1951 and 1953, and was on his way to a third in 1956 before he was injured in a race.

◆ **Curtis Turner**—A hard-partying, highly skilled driver, known especially for his prowess on dirt tracks, Turner was a star in the 1950s and 1960s. Besides his off-track reputation, Turner is most remembered for some of the races he didn't win.

*(Courtesy of T. Taylor Warren.)*

*Curtis Turner after winning a race.*

◆ **Joe Weatherly**—Another hard-partying racer nicknamed "Little Joe," Weatherly was a great racer with a fun reputation who finally won a championship in 1962. He and Curtis Turner had a saying that they may have lost the race, but they never lost the party.

## Great Moments

◆ The first field of strictly stock cars raced on June 19, 1949, at the Charlotte Fairgrounds. Glenn Dunnaway won the race but he was disqualified for using modified rear springs. Jim Roper was declared the winner.

◆ The first Southern 500 was held on September 4, 1950, at the brand new Darlington Raceway. The track was paved, more than a mile long, and featured high banks that attracted 75 racers to that Labor Day event.

◆ The first Daytona 500 was held on February 22, 1959, and wasn't decided until three days of study of a photo finish between Lee Petty and Johnny Beauchamp revealed that Petty had won.

# 1960 to 1969

Change in NASCAR in the 1960s came in the form of new racetracks, safety improvements, and the continued evolution of the car. The small dirt tracks were disappearing and being replaced by a new breed of paved superspeedways, a mile or longer, that changed the face of racing.

## Great Drivers and NASCharacters

◆ **Ned Jarrett**—He won a championship in 1961 and 1965. In 1965, he won 13 times. He retired in 1966 and is also known as popular race broadcaster and as Dale Jarrett's father.

◆ **Junior Johnson**—He was very good on the new superspeedways, and he won the 1960 Daytona 500 along with many other races. He was plowing a field behind a mule when his brother asked him to race in his place. From there, a legendary career was launched.

◆ **Fred Lorenzen**—He was known for his good looks as well as his ability to drive on the new superspeedways. In 1963, he had six victories and 23 top-ten finishes in 29 starts.

**Awesome!**

In 1969, Leroy Yarbrough had a great year on the superspeedways by winning twice at Daytona, twice at Darlington, and once at Atlanta. But then he had a bad crash, and later contracted Rocky Mountain spotted fever. After retiring, he was in the news in 1980 for trying to kill his mother. He was acquitted by reason of insanity.

- **David Pearson**—The great rival of Richard Petty, Pearson is considered one of the top drivers in history. He was Rookie of the Year in 1961, and the champion in 1966, 1968, and 1969. He is in second place in all-time wins.

- **Richard Petty**—The son of Lee Petty, Richard won races in the 1950s, 1960s, 1970s, and 1980s. He was the most dominating driver with the most victories, most wins in a season, and most consecutive wins. He was nicknamed "The King," and is the greatest driver and ambassador for the sport.

## Great Moments

- The 1963 Daytona 500 was won by Dewayne "Tiny" Lund on a single set of tires. He drove the Wood Brothers' car after saving fellow driver Marvin Panch from a burning car a few days before the race. Panch was supposed to drive, and the Wood Brothers rewarded Lund for saving Panch. Lund rewarded them with a victory.

- The 1965 Southern 500 was won by an astonishing 14 laps by Ned Jarrett. Driver Cale Yarborough survived a spectacular crash over a guardrail, and then he waved at the crowd and walked away.

- In 1967, Richard Petty won ten races in a row.

- Talladega opened in 1969, and the very first race was run by replacement drivers since the stars of the day boycotted, fearing for their safety on the new 2.66-mile superspeedway.

# 1970 to 1979

The era started out with the aerodynamic super cars while the big sponsor, Winston, joined on. By the end of the decade the Daytona 500 was broadcast live and in its entirety. The modern era had begun.

Richard Petty and David Pearson continued their epic battles but now new drivers were entering the evolving sport.

## Great Drivers and NASCharacters

◆ **Bobby Allison**—He was NASCAR's most popular driver in the early 1970s, finally winning a title in 1983.

◆ **Donnie Allison**—Bobby's younger brother won at Talladega in 1971 and 1977.

◆ **Janet Guthrie**—The first and most successful female driver of the modern television era (there were a few female drivers in the early years). She raced in a cup car off and on from 1976 to 1980. Her highest finish was sixth, at Bristol. She also raced in the Indianapolis 500.

◆ **H.A. "Humpy" Wheeler**—Hired in 1975 as the president and general manager of Lowe's Motor Speedway in Charlotte, Wheeler's innovative approach to promotion won him the nickname, "Racing's P.T. Barnum."

◆ **Benny Parsons**—He won the championship in 1973 and the Daytona 500 in 1975. He was the first driver to pass 200 mph in qualifying for the 1982 Winston 500 at Talladega. He went on to become a legendary broadcaster.

◆ **Cale Yarborough**—He was already a star in the 1960s, by winning the Daytona 500 and the Southern 500. He won three championships in a row, dominating 1976, 1977, and 1978.

## Great Moments

◆ On October 21, 1973, Benny Parsons captured the season championship by finishing just enough laps in a battered car to win the crown. His crew had to frantically repair the car to get him back on the track in the season's final race.

◆ 1976 Daytona 500—Considered by many to be the greatest race in the history of NASCAR, the race featured a wild finish between rivals Richard Petty and David Pearson. In the last 46 laps of the race, they traded the lead three times. And then as they came out of the final turn on the final lap, they crashed and spun into the infield. Petty couldn't restart his car but Pearson had kept the clutch down, so he kept the engine running and managed to roll over the finish line at about 25 mph.

*(Courtesy of Bill Niven.)*

*Richard Petty and David Pearson were fierce rivals on the track.*

◆ 1979 Daytona 500—The first live television broadcast of an entire race, a last-lap wreck, and a wild fight between Cale Yarborough and the Allison brothers—all captured on television (see Chapter 2).

# 1980 to 1989

New blood and charisma entered the sport, while the great Richard Petty was still around and getting big wins. Plus, NASCAR began showing up on the upstart network, ESPN.

In addition, the cars kept getting faster and a horrible accident at Talladega (see Chapter 2) caused a 1988 mandate that a restrictor plate be used at both Daytona and Talladega.

## Great Drivers and NASCharacters

- **Dale Earnhardt**—Won the first of seven championships in 1980. Known as "The Intimidator" for his refuse-to-lose driving style, he was one of the best and probably the most popular drivers in history. He famously drove the black "3" car. He died in a crash in the final lap of the 2001 Daytona 500. His father, Ralph Earnhardt, was also a great driver. His son, Dale Jr., is now the most popular driver.

- **Bill Elliott**—He was the 1988 champion. In 1985, by winning at three of NASCAR's four main tracks, he won a million dollars from Winston and earned the nickname "Million Dollar Bill."

- **Terry Labonte**—He won the championship in 1984 and 1996. His younger brother is Bobby Labonte, the 2000 champion.

- **Tim Richmond**—He was charismatic driver with a fast lifestyle. He won seven races in 1986. He died of complications from AIDS in 1989.

- **Rusty Wallace**—He was Rookie of the Year in 1984 and won the 1989 championship. He won 55 cup races in his career and now owns a Busch Series car driven by his son, Steve.

- **Darrell Waltrip**—He won three championships in the 1980s. He had great talent and the ability to tell everyone all about it. He was a tremendous self-promoter and then he backed up all of his words. He is now a television race announcer.

## Great Moments

- The 1984 Firecracker 400 at Daytona was Richard Petty's final victory. President Ronald Reagan attended the event with Bill France Sr. and saw Petty beat Cale Yarborough by inches for his 200th win.

◆ The 1987 Winston All-Star Race featured a wild battle between Geoffrey Bodine, Bill Elliott, and Dale Earnhardt as Earnhardt, in the lead, was forced into the tri-oval grass and maintained control, getting back onto the track while maintaining the lead. The maneuver, though not actually a pass, has been known since as "the pass in the grass." After the race, during the cool down lap, an angry Elliott confronted Earnhardt, cut him off, and then even ran his car into Earnhardt's.

**Awesome!**

When Alan Kulwicki won his first cup race at Phoenix in 1988, he drove a victory lap in the wrong direction (clockwise) around the race. He called the reverse-direction lap "my Polish Victory lap." He used it again in 1992 when he won the championship. Today, many drivers, especially those who knew Kulwicki, drive the Polish Victory lap in his honor.

◆ The 1988 Daytona 500 was won by Bobby Allison while his son, Davey, finished second. The two waved to each other just after crossing the finish line.

◆ The 1989 Winston All-Star race featured a turning point in Darrell Waltrip's career. Waltrip, a villain to many up to that point, became a sympathetic figure when Rusty Wallace spun out Waltrip to win the race. After the race, there was a fight between the two crews.

# 1990 to 1999

The modern era became the really modern era as mainstream America suddenly discovered NASCAR in a big way.

On the track, Dale Earnhardt dominated the beginning of the decade by winning four championships in five years. Jeff Gordon, a young kid from California, who arrived in NASCAR via Indiana, dominated the second half of the decade.

## Great Drivers and NASCharacters

◆ **Jeff Gordon**—He won championships in 1995, 1997, and 1998. He is one of the most successful and controversial figures in NASCAR history. As a California-born driver who learned in Indiana, Gordon is an outsider to traditional NASCAR. Some fans love him. Others hate him. He wins a lot, and he has a "Madison Avenue" appeal to advertisers that turns off some fans.

◆ **Dale Jarrett**—He won the championship in 1999. He is the son of two-time champion Ned Jarrett. He won the 1993 and 1996 Daytona 500.

◆ **Alan Kulwicki**—He won the championship in 1992. The inventor of the Polish Victory lap was killed in a plane crash on April 1, 1993.

## Great Moments

◆ The 1992 Hooters 500 in Atlanta was the last race of Richard Petty's career, and the first race of Jeff Gordon's.

◆ The 1994 Brickyard 400 was the first NASCAR race at the Indianapolis Motor Speedway, home to traditional racing and the Indianapolis 500. Jeff Gordon, who did much of his early racing in Indiana and was considered a hometown hero, won the race.

◆ Dale Earnhardt won his first Daytona 500 in 1998 after years of winning almost everything else. Crewmembers from every team lined pit road to congratulate the highly respected driver.

# 2000 to 2007

Everything changed when Dale Earnhardt died on the final lap of the 2001 Daytona 500. The tragic day made NASCAR into Page One news of newspaper and magazines. Television news featured it prominently. Earnhardt was mourned like a hero and all of America noticed.

And then, when the mourning faded, eyes stayed focused on NASCAR. It was bigger than ever.

## Great Drivers and NASCharacters

◆ **Kurt Busch**—He is the 2004 champion. He came to NASCAR from the bright lights of Las Vegas and has been accused of not respecting the history of the sport. But when he won the championship in 2004, he became part of that history.

◆ **Bobby Labonte**—He won the 2000 championship. He is the brother of Terry Labonte. He ran his first full season in 1993 and lost the Rookie of the Year award to Jeff Gordon.

◆ **Jimmie Johnson**—He is the 2006 champion and a teammate of Jeff Gordon, who is partial owner of Johnson's car. Johnson is one of the new well-spoken great drivers that have talent and charisma to succeed at all aspects of the modern sport.

◆ **Matt Kenseth**—He won the championship in 2003. He uses a smart points-gaining strategy of staying on the track when everyone else pits to allow himself to gain an extra five points for leading at least one lap of a race.

◆ **Tony Stewart**—He won the championship in 2002 and 2005. He is a tough, smart driver who is outspoken and very popular but sometimes gets in trouble with authority, like the time in 2007 when he compared NASCAR to professional wrestling.

## Great Moments

◆ The 2001 Pepsi 400 was won by Dale Earnhardt Jr. It was the first cup race held at Daytona International Speedway since Dale's father was killed at the 2001 Daytona 500 in February. It featured a memorable post-race celebration.

◆ The 2003 Carolina Dodge Dealers 400 featured a bang-'em-up last lap duel between Kurt Busch and Ricky Craven that ended with Craven winning by .002 seconds.

# Driving Families

When people say NASCAR is like family, they sometimes literally mean it. It starts, of course, with NASCAR itself—run by the France family. Brian France, NASCAR chairman, is the grandson of NASCAR founder Bill France Sr.

Here are some of the other family names that have had more than one famous name in the sport.

◆ Allison

◆ Earnhardt

◆ Hamilton

◆ Jarrett

◆ Labonte

◆ Marlin

◆ Petty

◆ Waltrip

◆ Wallace

# Earnhardt and Gordon/Waltrip

Every fan seems to have a favorite driver plus one they really don't like. And some drivers seem to rile up fans more than others. As always, perspective explains everything.

The truth about NASCAR, as in every other sport, is that some competitors are just plain better than others. Those are the ones that attract attention. And in the modern television era since the famous 1979 Daytona 500 (see Chapter 2), there have been three dominant champions.

None has been more dominant than the late Dale Earnhardt, who won seven championships between 1980 and 1994. With a trademark bushy mustache, black "3" car, and a tough, take-no-prisoners driving style, Earnhardt, of North Carolina, has been called a "working man's driver." His aura as a symbol of ... again, pick your perspective ... was summed up in a label that must have been a marketer's dream: *The Intimidator.* Most of Earnhardt's fans, the biggest fan base in NASCAR, now root for his son, Dale Jr.

Darrell Waltrip was a superstar who let everybody know it and then backed everything up by winning the championship three times in five years in the early 1980s. He was a trash-talking, charismatic, get-on-the-nerves Hollywood kind of winner from Kentucky that America loves to love, and loves to hate. And he knew it. Many hated him. *Hated.*

That brings us to Jeff Gordon, one of the most controversial figures in modern NASCAR. And it's bizarre because Gordon himself is not controversial. The fans have made him so. To understand why Gordon is controversial, you first have to consider the stories of Waltrip as an outsider in the sport from Kentucky and that of Earnhardt, who, after his death in 2001, has achieved something akin to NASCAR sainthood.

*(Courtesy of Mike Horne.)*

*Dale Earnhardt and Jeff Gordon were fierce rivals on the track.*

Lots of fans, especially Earnhardt fans, think that Jeff Gordon never seemed to pay any dues. He came into cup racing and immediately started winning. Between 1994 and 2001, he won four championships and he remains one of the top cup car drivers. As an outsider, the California-born, Indiana-trained Gordon brought many new fans with him into what was still mostly a regional sport.

He was not only a tremendous driver, but he had a Hollywood type of polished appeal that landed him in places where no NASCAR driver has ever gone before. He hosted Saturday Night Live and co-hosted morning talk shows. His shiny polish—many think too shiny—along with his on-track success and his outsider status have made him a hero to many and a villain to many others.

That just begins to explain the most fascinating modern plot in the world's fastest soap opera.

When it seemed the plot couldn't get any more interesting, on Wednesday June 13, 2007, it did. On that day Dale Earnhardt Jr., who had been driving for his father's company, Dale Earnhardt Incorporated, announced he was moving for the 2008 season (and beyond) to the team owned by Rick Hendrick. Hendrick already has a couple of famous drivers on his team.

In a who-could-believe-it twist, Dale Earnhardt Jr., whose fans have a serious dislike for Jeff Gordon, is about to be teammates with Jeff Gordon. Also on the team is two-time champion Jimmie Johnson. You want interesting? NASCAR gives you interesting.

## The Least You Need to Know

- ◆ Richard Petty won the most; David Pearson won the second most championships.

- ◆ The battle between Petty and Pearson in the 1976 Daytona 500 is considered by many as the greatest race of all time.

- ◆ Dale Earnhardt, a fan favorite known as "The Intimidator" won seven championships. He died in a crash in 2001. Most of his fans now root for his son, Dale Earnhardt Jr.

- ◆ Jeff Gordon has won four championships, and counting.

- ◆ Fans seem to either love or hate Jeff Gordon.

# NASCAR as a Cultural Phenomenon

## In This Chapter

◆ Clues that NASCAR is everywhere

◆ NASCAR at the movies

◆ NASCAR in music

◆ NASCAR on television

◆ NASCAR in politics

◆ Souvenirs

The United States of America is a NASCAR nation. From North Carolina to California—yes, from sea to shining sea—television sets glow and racetracks roar with NASCAR's spectacular stock car traveling show.

But NASCAR is bigger than the events themselves. It is a cultural phenomenon and more—a world of movies and cartoons and commercials and even rocking chairs with steering wheels for the older fan.

As a marketing tool and a mindset, NASCAR has forced or charmed (sold) its way onto many products on the country's store shelves and, in fact, all the way into the culture and psyche of the melting pot that is America.

The word *NASCAR* is American shorthand for ... whatever you want it to mean but it means something—something definite and real and a lot more than simply the acronym for the National Association of Stock Car Automobile Racing.

This is a chapter about some of the things that are all-things-NASCAR, the things that don't necessarily have to do with anything on the track. There are too many to name and someone is probably coming up with a new way to make money off of NASCAR as you are reading this paragraph.

This chapter will cover some of the highlights, such as movies, music, television, print, and the Internet. It will touch on the role NASCAR has played in politics, how NASCAR has reached out to women, and it will discuss the many available NASCAR souvenirs.

# NASCAR Is Everywhere ...

Hungry? How about some candy? Thirsty? Do you like beer or soda? Oh heck, none of that. You just want to fix up your house, right? Well, no matter what you want to do in America, there's no escaping NASCAR. Not that you'd ever want to get away from NASCAR, but if you did want to get away, you couldn't.

Do you have a favorite star from anywhere—the movies, a singer, or the like—in popular culture? Well, there's a good chance that he or she likes NASCAR and is planning to sing the National Anthem or maybe give the command, "Gentleman, start your engines" at a race sometime soon.

Have you ever watched television and seen an advertisement? Drivers are all over the TV these days. Yes, NASCAR—and especially the drivers—are everywhere and the products are just as prevalent.

Do you want a NASCAR guitar? Of course you do. But first, let's go to the movies.

# NASCAR at the Movies

The camera loves a fast car and that's one of a million reasons why NASCAR is popular on television (more later). And for years Hollywood has been trying, with varying success, to capture the drama of real NASCAR.

Here are two (probably incomplete, all apologies) lists of stars that have appeared in a fictional or biographical fiction movie that was somehow about NASCAR:

Movie stars: Ned Beaty, Jeff Bridges, Gary Busey, James Caan, Rory Calhoun, Sacha Baron Cohen, Tom Cruise, Matt Dillon, Robert Duvall, Will Ferrell, Alan Hale Jr., Lindsey Lohan, Michael Keaton, Nicole Kidman, Darren McGavin, Jim Nabors, Elvis Presley, Richard Petty (Playing himself in "43: The Richard Petty Story"), Richard Pryor, Burt Reynolds, Nancy Sinatra, George Takei.

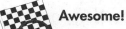

**Awesome!**

The 1968 movie, "Speedway" stars Elvis Presley, the king of rock and roll, and includes a cameo by Richard Petty. That's right—it features The King and The King.

NASCAR driver cameos on film: Buck Baker, Jeff Gordon, Tiny Lund, Richard Petty, Curtis Turner, Rusty Wallace, Joe Weatherly, Cale Yarborough, Dale Earnhardt. Earnhardt had a cameo in the movie *Baseketball* from the creators of South Park.

Here is a list of some movies about NASCAR: *Cars, Dale, 3: The Dale Earnhardt Story, Days of Thunder, 43: The Richard Petty Story, Greased Lightning, Herbie: Fully Loaded, The Last American Hero, NASCAR 3-D: The IMAX Experience, Redline 7000, Six Pack, Speedway, Stroker Ace, Talladega Nights: The Ballad of Ricky Bobby,* and *Thunder in Carolina.*

*(Courtesy of Bryan Hallman.)*

*Will Ferrell in Talledega Nights: The Ballad of Ricky Bobby.*

In addition to fictional movies starring humans, there has been one fictional movie, *Cars,* starring animated cars and featuring the voices of Paul Newman, Owen Wilson, Larry the Cable Guy, Cheech Marin, Tony Shalhoub, and Bonnie Hunt. It also featured cameo voices by stars such as Jay Leno and drivers like Dale Earnhardt Jr.

In addition, there has been more than one NASCAR documentary and almost all the current stars sell some version of their own life story DVD.

One other movie is important. *NASCAR 3-D: The IMAX Experience.* Narrated by Kiefer Sutherland, this 47-minute documentary is a put-you-there experience.

# NASCAR and Music

Rock and roll and NASCAR are parallel outlaw entities beginning in the 1950s. But that's only part of the story of the relationship between music and NASCAR.

That's right—gimme three chords and start your engines, because NASCAR and music go together like the Southern rock band Lynyrd Skynyrd goes with their sweet home state of Alabama. The crossroads where Alabama's Lynyrd Skynyrd meets Michigan's Bob Seger is a good place to start looking for the unofficial music of NASCAR.

The more official place to look would be Cherry Lane Publishing, which teamed up with NASCAR to create something called "Motor Music." According to Cherry Lane's website, "This music has the fast moving, rough, tough, down, and dirty feel that makes your insides shake with excitement."

**Awesome!**

One weekly syndicated radio show, "Racing Rocks!" hosted by Riki Rachtman, mixes rock and roll with NASCAR by interspersing great songs with racing news and interviews.

In addition, in 2007, NASCAR teamed up with American Idol and recording artist Kelly Clarkson to do numerous NASCAR appearances including concerts at the track, in television advertisements, and at the Nextel Cup awards ceremony.

She is also helping promote the annual NASCAR day, which raises awareness of the sport as well as raises money for the charitable NASCAR Foundation. Like most NASCAR deals, it is designed as a win-win: Clarkson helps NASCAR and the exposure helps Clarkson.

One more important note: before a race the national anthem is always played and sung, often by a celebrity singer.

# NASCAR on TV

NASCAR on television is worth billions (see Chapter 10) because it is so popular. The various series are shown on a combination of channels including Fox, SPEED, ESPN/ABC, and TNT.

**Awesome!**

The legendary racer Darrell Waltrip is now a race announcer. He begins each race he announces, as the green flag is dropped, with the words, *"Boogity, boogity, boogity—let's go racin' boys!"*

The races are popular and now there is more to watch than just the races. There is a channel, SPEED, dedicated to motorsports. In addition, ESPN broadcasts a news and analysis show called "NASCAR Now."

**Awesome!**

One of the analysts on NASCAR Now is seven-foot- tall Brad Daugherty, who had a legendary career playing basketball for the Cleveland Cavaliers. Daugherty, a lifelong race fan, wore number 43 in the NBA in honor of his favorite driver, Richard Petty.

But NASCAR is not just about the racing or the news of the racing. One show that is still rebroadcast on certain cable channels is the 2000 animated kids series, NASCAR Racers, featuring the good team, Fastex, against the evil team, Rexcor.

And, of course, television commercials are featuring more NASCAR drivers every year as they become integrated into the overall branding of a company.

Finally, NASCAR is never an entity to be left behind in any trend, so it has entered the world of reality television on ABC, airing "Fast Cars and Superstars: Gillette Young Guns' Celebrity Race," featuring young drivers instructing celebrities on how to drive a race car. It aired during the 2007 NBA Finals week.

# NASCAR in Print and on the Internet

There are lots of websites about NASCAR. Here are two:

◆ NASCAR.com

◆ Jayski.com

There are also lots of publications about NASCAR. Here are two:

◆ NASCAR Scene

◆ Dick Berggren's Speedway Illustrated

# NASCAR and Politics

Ronald Reagan was the first sitting president to visit a NASCAR race. Since then, politicians have noticed that fans vote.

And since politics loves to use shorthand and sound bytes, the 2004 presidential election produced a new term, NASCAR dads—meaning, well, male NASCAR fans with kids.

Somehow the discovery of NASCAR dads seemed to be the media's way to counterbalance that other powerful group it once created, soccer moms— you know, women with kids that play soccer.

**Awesome!** _____

In the 2004 presidential election, the Republican Party was serious about NASCAR dads. It sent an 18-wheel vehicle dubbed "Reggie the Registration Rig" to NASCAR events trying to register voters.

# NASCAR and Women

Forty percent of NASCAR fans are women. NASCAR knows all about it and is focusing on women with specialty items such as shoes with small, checkered flags as part of the design.

But one of the most interesting of all NASCAR products was the 2006 introduction of NASCAR-based Harlequin (romance) novels. The first book in the series was called, "In the Groove," by Pamela Britton.

# Race City USA

In America, NASCAR might be anywhere, but if you want to find where NASCAR is everywhere, the place to go is Mooresville, North Carolina.

**Awesome!** _____

Besides the races, one special treat travels the country for race fans to enjoy. Fans can actually drive, or ride in, a NASCAR-type vehicle with The Richard Petty Driving Experience. See www.1800bepetty.com to find a track near you.

Located about 25 miles north of Charlotte, this is home to many race teams and museums, including Dale Earnhardt Inc.'s famous 70,000-square foot Garage Mahal.

# Souvenirs

From cradle to grave, you can be a NASCAR fan—even turning left all the way to heaven in your special casket.

But before you leave Earth, you'll need some souvenirs. You need a t-shirt and you might even want to get to a track and buy a used tire—yes, a tire. Listen up—tires are cool. And yes, a tattoo would be awesome but maybe you just want the belt buckle or, if you are female, perhaps some NASCAR earrings and underwear.

How about NASCAR posters, trading cards, hats, curtains, or bed sheets? If you want it, you can get it and if you can't get it you might be able to (with NASCAR's permission) make and sell it and find a whole bunch more people just like you who want—no, need—to have that certain something.

**Awesome!**

Die-cast cars that look and are painted exactly as cup cars are probably the most popular collectible. They cost up to $80 each, and most fans who collect them have more than one.

If you were born today, you can start with a NASCAR pacifier and then live a long life and end up in the rocking chair with a steering wheel, but not before first playing some guitar, featuring your favorite driver's number and color scheme.

So here's your plan: start your engine and rock on, and then turn left and rock on some more in your rocking chair.

## The Least You Need to Know

◆ Look around and you will see something to do with NASCAR.

◆ Cameras love a fast car.

◆ Music and NASCAR go together.

◆ Race fans love to collect die-cast cars.

◆ You can probably buy a NASCAR-themed anything.

# Glossary

**big one**   Refers to the almost inevitable multiple-car pileup that happens, especially at the long superspeedways of Talladega and Daytona. Cars are so close together that when a crash happens, sometimes more than 20 cars are involved.

**bump and run**   Occurs usually at small tracks, especially Bristol and Martinsville. This technique involves a trailing car bumping the back bumper of the leading car just enough so that the lead driver has to struggle to regain control. Meanwhile, the trailing driver cruises right past him.

**bump drafting**   A controversial technique of intentionally ramming into the back bumper of the car in front of you to speed both cars up. Many drivers are asking that bump drafting be banned from NASCAR.

**Buschwhackers**   Is a term for Nextel Cup drivers who also drive in the Busch series.

**Daytona Beach Course**   Was the original stretch of Ormond Beach in Daytona where many land speed records were set. From the earliest part of the century, racers came to Daytona Beach like a racing Mecca, because at low tide it provided a long stretch of hard sand where you could go really fast.

**Daytona Beach and Road Course** Was an oval racetrack (it has since been replaced) that started on Route A1A, turned left onto the hard sands of Daytona Beach, and then turned back onto Route A1A. The original length was 3.2 miles, but it was lengthened to 4.2 miles in the 1940s. It closed in 1959.

**development driver** Is the name for a driver who is in the system and trying to earn the right to drive a cup car.

**drafting** Occurs in restrictor plate (see Chapter 6) racing at Talladega and Daytona. Drivers know that two cars together, because of the aero-dynamics, go faster than one car alone. Therefore drivers need partners to team up with and then they have to be cold-hearted enough to break away from the partner when it is time to win.

**Grand Prix** Means grand prize. In Formula One racing, the Grand Prix is the premier race in any given nation. The first Grand Prix was held in Le Mans, France in 1906.

**HANS device** Is a Head and Neck Support device, a collar that is harnessed to the upper body. The collar is then attached to the helmet with two flexible tethers that allow the head some flexibility to drive but prevent it from snapping forward during a wreck.

**hitting the marks** Is what a driver is trying to do around each turn, which is hit a certain spot on the racetrack on the way into the turn and on the way out. This assures consistency throughout the turn.

**indexing a tire** Is what a tire carrier does to line up the lug nut holes with the lug nuts. He visually indexes it to find exactly where every-thing is so he can slip the tire on smoothly on the first try.

**loose** Is a condition of turning. A car is loose in a turn when, as it goes around the turn, the back end wants to slide out of control. The phenomenon of loose is much like a car going down a snowy street, turning the wheel sideways and sliding sideways down the street.

**lucky dog** Is the car one lap down that is the closest to the lead lap when the caution flag comes out. That car automatically gets the lap back unless it is during the final ten laps of the race.

**restrictor plate** Is used to reduce horsepower on the superspeedways of Daytona and Talladega.

**setup**   The description of how the many variables—such as shocks and springs and chassis adjustments—are set on a car is before and during a race.

**spotter**   Is a person placed high above the racetrack with a radio who serves as a second set of eyes for the driver. The spotter can see the whole track with something of a helicopter view and alert the driver to many situations including crashes, faster drivers approaching, or other drivers dueling in front of him.

**start/finish line**   Is the checkered line that signals where cars start and is also where the race ends—thus, the name.

**tight**   Is a condition of turning. A car is tight when it goes into the turn and the car tends to want to go straight instead of flow into the turn.

**track bar**   Connects the rear end to the chassis and prevents the chassis from swaying side to side. The height of this attachment has a lot to do with whether the car is loose or tight. Lowering the track bar will make the car tighter, and raising it will make it looser.

**tradin' paint**   Occurs when two cars bump but don't have a major collision. Often, there is actually paint from one car on the body of the other.

**Victory Lane**   Is where the winning racecar is taken after a race to celebrate and get presented with some kind of reward.

**wheelbase**   Is the distance between the center of the front wheel and the center of the rear wheel.

**zipper top cars**   Were convertibles that could easily be converted into hardtop stock cars. There was no zipper. The top was bolted on.

# Index

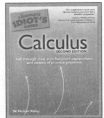